Amphibians, Reptiles, and Their Conservation

AMPHIBIANS, REPTILES,

AND THEIR

CONSERVATION

by
Marty Crump

LINNET BOOKS

North Haven, Connecticut

Library of Congress Cataloging-in-Publication Data

Crump, Marty
  Amphibians, reptiles, and their conservation / by Marty Crump.
    p. cm.
  Includes bibliographical references (p.).
  Summary: Provides an overview of amphibians and reptiles, discussing common
perceptions about these species, phobias, how humans impact their survival, and more.
  ISBN 0-208-02511-1 (alk. paper)
   1. Amphibians—Juvenile literature. 2. Reptiles—Juvenile literature. 3. Wildlife
conservation—Juvenile literature. [1. Amphibians. 2. Reptiles. 3. Wildlife conservation.]
I. Title.

QL644.2 .C78 2002
597.9—dc21

                                                      2002073072

All photographs were taken by Marty Crump unless otherwise noted.

Designed and drawings by Carol Sawyer of Rose Design

Printed in Hong Kong by C & C Offset Printing Co., Ltd.

For Clark, Séamas, and all children,
for they hold the future of amphibians and reptiles
in their hands.

Contents

Acknowledgments

While writing a chapter on the conservation of amphibians and reptiles for the college textbook *Herpetology*, I thought, "Why not share this information with kids?" After all, they are the generation that will have a major impact on the future of amphibians and reptiles. They will be the voters of tomorrow. They will set the policies of tomorrow. And they will raise the children of tomorrow. Thus, I'm grateful to Harvey Pough for inviting me to be a coauthor of the *Herpetology* textbook, which ultimately inspired me to write this book.

Many people read the manuscript for this book and offered valuable suggestions for improvement. For their help I thank Annie Crego and her students Michael Blancarte (5th grade) and Natasha Slaughter (6th grade); Darcie Whitney and her students Ben Bennett and Peter Bremer (both 7th graders) and Jennifer Dunn and Holland Wilberger (both 8th graders); Karen Feinsinger, Judy Hendrickson, and Jenny Vollman. Special thanks go to my husband, Peter Feinsinger, who not only supported my endeavors, but greatly improved my prose.

I thank Diantha Thorpe and Colleen Spata from Linnet Books for believing in this book and for their guidance and support.

TOO WEIRD TO BE TRUE?

They come in every color of the rainbow and more: rose, lemon yellow, tangerine, lavender, sky blue, jungle green, chocolate, ebony, and ivory. They eat just about everything, from food the size of algae and bacteria to water buffalo. They range in size from smaller than 1 inch to more than 25 feet. They live on land, underground, high in the trees, in the ocean, and in ponds, lakes, and rivers. They walk, run, hop, crawl, climb, slither, glide, and swim. What are they? They're amphibians and reptiles.

These animals are generally less well-known and understood than are birds and mammals. They're just as fascinating, though. For example . . .

APPEARANCE

Some amphibians and reptiles are spectacularly colored. Although most bullfrogs are green, some are blue. Several kinds

1

of salamanders are bright red with black spots. Chameleons not only have yellow-orange, vermilion, violet, turquoise, and emerald green spots, they can also change their colors depending on their moods: Some male chameleons become much brighter when they court females or confront other males. Painted turtles look as though someone took a brush and went wild painting the shells with stripes and splotches of green, yellow, orange, and black. Common mussurana snakes change color as they get older: Juveniles are red with black snouts and white neckbands; adults are shiny black except for their cream-colored undersides.

Some amphibians and reptiles have amazing bodies that seem too weird to be true. Horned treefrogs, with their bizarre-shaped triangular heads, look like creatures from another planet. Surinam toads mimic burnt, four-legged pancakes. Amphiuma salamanders paddle through the water on four ridiculously tiny legs. Matamata turtles snorkel above the surface of rivers with their long, fleshy Pinocchio-like snouts. Flying dragon lizards glide through the air by spreading out flaps of skin along the sides of their bodies. Vine snakes can balance their 2-foot-long, skinny bodies on your finger.

DEFENSE

Amphibians and reptiles protect themselves from predators in clever ways. Horned lizards squirt blood from the corners of their eyes. Spitting cobras spit venom and aim for the eyes of their attackers. Toads often urinate when bothered, and garter snakes often defecate when grabbed by predators. Some gecko lizards and salamanders spray or ooze sticky secretions from their tails onto predators. While the predator tries to disentangle itself, the gecko or salamander escapes.

Toxic chemicals of some amphibians and reptiles can sicken or kill predators. *Poisonous** animals, for example some frogs and salamanders, have toxins that are secreted from skin glands. If a predator tries to eat the frog or salamander, it gets a mouthful of poisonous slime. Most poisonous amphibians won't hurt you unless you rub your eyes after handling them, or unless the toxin gets into a cut. *Venomous* snakes, for example coral snakes, have toxin glands in their mouths. Teeth or fangs connected to these glands inject the toxin into another animal.

Many poisonous and venomous animals are brightly colored. These colors warn would-be predators against eating, or even bothering, the animal. Poison dart frogs, in shades of blue, purple, green, orange, yellow, and red, warn: "Don't mess with me. I'm poisonous." Fire salamanders convey the same message in vivid yellow and black. Flashy coral snakes warn with red, yellow, and black rings.

Cobras spread their hoods in a threat display, and rattlesnakes shake their rattles to warn intruders. When attacked, hog-nosed snakes roll over, go limp, and play dead—usually with their tongues hanging out of their open mouths. Some treefrogs also roll over onto their backs and play dead. A predator hoping to eat the snake or frog may not eat dead animals, so it drops its catch. Many kinds of salamanders and lizards purposely let part of their tails break off when they're grabbed by predators. The predator focuses its attention on the tail that's still wiggling, allowing the salamander or lizard to escape.

If nothing else works, some amphibians and reptiles fight back by biting, clawing, or smacking their tails against their attacker.

---

* Italicized words are defined in the glossary.

CARE FOR THEIR YOUNG

Although most amphibians abandon their eggs, some are terrific parents. Mother marsupial treefrogs carry their fertilized eggs in pouches on their backs. Some mother and father dink frogs stand guard to protect their eggs from spiders and other predators. Frog parents can be feisty! Father gladiator frogs from Panama defend their eggs from other males by wrestling and digging sharp thumb spines into their opponents' eyes and ears. Some frog parents hiss and lunge at predators that try to eat their eggs.

Male Darwin's frogs from Chile and Argentina watch over their 3 to 8 fertilized eggs for about 20 days. When the eggs are just about ready to hatch, Dad slurps them into his mouth. From there the eggs slip down into his *vocal sac*, the balloon-like pouch in the throat area that fills with air when a male frog calls. The eggs soon hatch into tadpoles. Dad carries his tadpoles in his vocal sac until the babies metamorphose (transform or change) into little frogs about 50 days later. Then, Dad opens his mouth, and the little frogs hop out.

Some reptiles, too, care for their kids. Mother alligators and crocodiles usually stay near the nests after they lay their eggs. They chase and bite intruders. When the young are about ready to hatch, they peep, yelp, and grunt. This attracts Mom's attention. She rips open the nest and may carry the babies in her mouth to water. Mom stays near her young, sometimes for a year or more, and protects them from predators until they grow large enough to protect themselves. Even the father sometimes helps defend his eggs and later his youngsters.

Some snakes are also caring parents. Females of several kinds of pythons coil around their eggs. By twitching their bodies they contract their muscles and generate heat to warm the eggs. Female African forest cobras lay their eggs in nests of leaves and decaying vegetation. Both the mother and the father will guard the nest.

FOOD AND FOOD-GETTING BEHAVIOR

The variety of food eaten by amphibians and reptiles can make our meals seem boring. Some eat mushrooms or plants such as flowers, leaves, berries and other fruit, or seaweed. Others eat worms, insects, and even tarantulas and scorpions. Those with large mouths feast on larger prey—fishes, other amphibians and reptiles, birds, and mammals. Narrow-mouth toads and horned lizards eat mainly ants and termites. Goo-eater snakes prefer slugs and snails.

African egg-eating snakes swallow bird eggs that are three times the width of their heads. That's equivalent to you swallowing a large watermelon—whole! The snake crushes the shell in its throat, swallows the inside of the egg, and then vomits up the shell.

Many amphibians and reptiles actively search for their prey. Others lie in wait for insects cruising by. Komodo dragons, which can be 10 feet long and weigh up to 330 pounds, ambush small deer, wild boar, and even water buffalo.

"Pac-man" frogs have mouths so big they look like hopping mouths with legs attached. They eat other frogs, lizards, and even baby birds and mice. A pac-man frog will sometimes twitch its long, skinny toe to mimic a moving insect. When a frog hops over to check out the possible meal, the owner of the toe eats the frog instead.

Some reptiles also catch their dinners by trickery. An alligator snapping turtle opens its mouth and wiggles a worm-like flap of skin on its tongue. When a fish swims into the mouth to eat the worm, the turtle eats the fish. A Saharan sand viper spends most of the day buried in the sand. Only its eyes and snout peek above the surface. If the snake detects a lizard nearby, it pokes its black-and-white banded tail above the sand and slowly wiggles it. When the lizard lunges at what it thinks is a meal, the snake strikes, injects venom into the lizard, and then eats it.

* * *

But all these interesting facts don't really tell us what sort of animals reptiles and amphibians are. For that, we need to dig deeper. We need to look at not only the unusual and bizarre animals, but the "everyday" ones as well.

WHAT ARE AMPHIBIANS AND REPTILES?

Herpetology is the study of amphibians and reptiles. The word comes from the Greek word *herpeton* meaning crawling thing and from *logos* meaning knowledge. But why are wet-to-the-touch salamanders and frogs lumped together with armored alligators and scaly rattlesnakes? The reason is that 200 years ago, people thought that the differences between amphibians and reptiles were relatively minor. They called all of them amphibians. Now we know that amphibians and reptiles are very different in many ways. It may not make much sense, but these animals are still grouped together. They're often called "herpetofauna," "herps," or "herptiles."

HOW ARE AMPHIBIANS AND REPTILES SIMILAR TO EACH OTHER?

All amphibians and reptiles have a skeleton called a backbone. The backbone is made up of individual structures of cartilage or bone, called vertebrae. Humans also have vertebrae, as do other mammals, birds, and fish. For this reason, all of these animals are called *vertebrates*. They belong to the subphylum Vertebrata (a subdivision of the phylum Chordata). Vertebrata is divided into several groups, called *classes*. We belong to the class Mammalia. Amphibians belong to the class Amphibia, and reptiles belong to the class Reptilia.

Backbones aren't the only feature that amphibians and reptiles share. Both groups of animals are *ectothermic*. That is, in order to get their body temperatures high enough to be active, they need an external (outside) source of heat to warm their bodies. This external source of heat is the sun. The animals either bask in the sun or rest on a warm surface, such as a rock or mud that the sun has warmed up.

Often amphibians and reptiles are said to be "cold-blooded," but ectothermic is a better term because on a warm day their blood isn't cold. Instead, their body temperature stays about the same as their surroundings. In the early morning a lizard is sluggish. It's cold (and its blood is cold) because the ground it sits on is cold. After the lizard basks in the sun for awhile, its body temperature warms up. The lizard scampers off and hunts for food. Later in the day, it may move into the shade because its body is too hot. Shuttling back and forth between sun and shade, and by seeking shelter, the lizard keeps its body at a good temperature.

Humans, other mammals, and birds are *endothermic*. These animals have built-in control of body temperature. Endotherms produce heat chemically, inside their bodies, by breaking down the food they eat. In this way they maintain a constant high body temperature. Because it takes a lot of energy to "keep the furnace

SCIENTIFIC CLASSIFICATION

Humans everywhere recognize and name different kinds of plants and animals. The Jivaro Indians of eastern Ecuador have individual names for each plant they consider edible, poisonous, or medicinal. Likewise the Masai people of Kenya, the Pygmies of the Congo River Basin, and the Bushmen of the Kalahari Desert have names for each plant and animal important to them—each in their own language.

Long ago, naturalists and scientists realized they needed a standard system of grouping and naming plants and animals so they could communicate with each other worldwide. They developed scientific classification, a way of grouping organisms in a hierarchical system. Organisms within a group are more similar to each other than they are to organisms that belong to other groups. So, what language is used? Latin and Greek, because the early scholars who classified organisms used these languages.

In 1753, Carolus Linnaeus, a Swedish naturalist, developed the scientific classification system we use today. There are 7 main levels in the Linnean hierarchy, though many are further broken down into subgroups. From highest to lowest, these are: kingdom, phylum, class, order, family, genus, and species.

We currently recognize 5 kingdoms. All animals belong to Animalia, the largest kingdom. The other 4 kingdoms include the plants, fungi, bacteria, and algae. Each kingdom is made up of groups called phyla (phylum, singular). Animalia consists of about 20 phyla. One of these is Chordata. All animals that have a notochord (a rod-like cord that runs down the body and provides support) during some stage of their lives are lumped together in the phylum Chordata. A major subgroup, or subphylum, of Chordata is Vertebrata—animals that have backbones made up of vertebrae. The approximately 45,000 living species of vertebrates are divided into 7 classes: Agnatha (jawless fishes, such as lamprey), Chondrichthyes (cartilaginous fishes, such as sharks), Osteichthyes (bony fishes, such as trout), Amphibia (amphibians, such as bullfrogs), Reptilia (reptiles, such as garter snakes), Aves (birds, such as robins), and Mammalia (mammals, such as dogs).

Each class is divided into orders. The class Amphibia consists of 3 orders: Anura (frogs and toads), Urodela (salamanders), and Gymnophiona (caecilians), as discussed in the next chapter. The fifth level is family. The order Anura consists of 27 recognized families. One is Ranidae, to which leopard frogs and bullfrogs belong. The sixth and seventh levels make up what we call binomial nomenclature. Each animal has a two-word name consisting of a genus (sixth level) and species (seventh level) name. There may be lots of species within a genus, but each has a separate species name. For example, leopard frogs are *Rana pipiens*. Bullfrogs are *Rana catesbeiana*. Notice that the genus and species names are italicized, and the genus name is capitalized. Following are some examples of the seven-part classification system.

	you	Komodo dragon	leopard frog	snapping turtle
Kingdom	Animalia	Animalia	Animalia	Animalia
Phylum	Chordata	Chordata	Chordata	Chordata
Class	Mammalia	Reptilia	Amphibia	Reptilia
Order	Primates	Squamata	Anura	Testudines
Family	Hominidae	Varanidae	Ranidae	Chelydridae
Genus	Homo	Varanus	Rana	Chelydra
Species	sapiens	komodoensis	pipiens	serpentina

going," birds and mammals need to eat a lot more than amphibians and reptiles. At least 90% of the energy you take in from food goes into maintaining your body temperature. The same goes for other endotherms. This means that less than 10% of the energy in food is left for growth or reproduction. In contrast, between 30% and 90% of the energy an amphibian or reptile gets from its food is used for growth or reproduction. Ectotherms and endotherms represent two very different ways of going about life.

HOW ARE AMPHIBIANS AND REPTILES DIFFERENT FROM EACH OTHER?

The most obvious difference between amphibians and reptiles is the nature of their skin. Reptiles have dry skin and scales that keep their bodies from losing moisture. Some can live in deserts and other dry places. Their scales are made of *keratin*, a protein also found in your fingernails and in birds' feathers. Instead of scales, an amphibian's skin is covered with mucus that's produced by glands. Some people don't like to touch amphibians because they're "slimy." Without the mucus, though, an amphibian on dry land might die. Amphibians do part of their breathing through their skin, but this only works if the skin is moist or wet.

Amphibians and reptiles also reproduce in different ways. Most amphibians, even many that live out of water as adults, lay their eggs in water and the eggs hatch into larvae. Amphibian eggs have several jelly capsules surrounding and protecting the embryo. The eggs of most frogs and toads hatch into larvae, called tadpoles or polliwogs. In salamanders and caecilians, the young are just called larvae. The larvae stay in the water until they metamorphose (change) into the body form of the adults.

This mass of frog eggs was attached to plants in the water. Each black egg is protected by jelly capsules.

In contrast, all reptiles, even the ones that spend most of their lives in water, lay their eggs on land. Why don't the eggs dry out? One reason is that inside the egg, a reptile embryo floats in its own fluid, surrounded by a membrane called the *amnion.* Another reason is that the outside of a reptile egg is covered with a shell that protects the embryo. Some reptile eggs have brittle shells, like birds' eggs; others have tough leathery shells. Tiny pores in the shell allow the embryo to breathe: Oxygen passes in to the embryo and carbon dioxide passes out. Unlike amphibians, baby reptiles don't go through *metamorphosis.* They just grow.

Not all amphibians and reptiles lay eggs, though. In some kinds of frogs, salamanders, caecilians, lizards, and snakes, the young develop inside the mother's body, and she gives birth to fully formed young just as most mammals do.

MEET THE AMPHIBIANS

The word amphibian comes from the Greek words *amphi* meaning double and *bios* meaning life. This is an appropriate name, because many amphibians live in the water and on land at different times of their lives. Most begin as eggs in water and end up as adults on land, but there are exceptions. Some amphibians are completely *aquatic* (live in the water), and others are entirely *terrestrial* (live on land) throughout their lives.

Scientists divide the class Amphibia into three groups, or *orders*. The largest order is the Anura, which consists of frogs and toads. Anura comes from the Greek words *an* and *oura* meaning "without tail." Adult frogs and toads don't have tails. Salamanders belong to the order Urodela, named from the Greek words *uro* and *delos* meaning "tail evident." All salamanders have tails—some short and fat, others long and skinny. The third order, unfamiliar to most people, is the Gymnophiona, the caecilians. Caecilians are long, thin, worm-like amphibians without legs. Gymnophiona comes from the Greek words *gymnos* and *ophis* meaning "naked serpent." Caecilians look like snakes without scales.

ORDER ANURA: FROGS AND TOADS

More *species,* or kinds, of frogs and toads exist than in the other two orders of amphibians combined. New species are discovered every year, especially in tropical areas of the world where there are still many unexplored places. Currently we think there are about 4300 species in total.

Adult frogs and toads have four legs, and they lack tails. Most have strong hind legs, well-suited for jumping. And there the similarities end. Body shapes range from pointed snouts connected to thin, long torsos to snub noses connected to ping-pong ball figures. There may be webs between the fingers and toes, or not. Some frogs are covered with warty bumps, each filled with poison. Others have smooth skin. Some have bony horns on their heads. Others have spines of skin on their noses, eyelids, or legs. People who say "a frog is a frog" haven't seen the diversity that exists.

Males of most frogs and toads call to attract females during the mating season. Each species has its own particular call, and females recognize and respond only to the calls given by males of their own species. Calls are more than just "ribbets" and "croaks"— they're grunts, peeps, trills, bonks, squawks, tinks, whistles, and clicks. Calls may be single notes, or groups of repeated notes. Some are melodious, others are downright irritating to the human eardrum. In a few species, females also have a voice, but their call is much softer than the male's call. These females use their voice to communicate to males just before mating.

What's the difference between frogs and toads? All toads are frogs but not all frogs are toads. Confused? Think about dogs. All poodles are dogs but not all dogs are poodles. Toads are one type of frog, and poodles are one type of dog. The word toad is usually used for frogs that have drier skin, squat and warty bodies, and hind legs that aren't very powerful. Toads tend to "flop" when they jump, in contrast to the clean, Olympic-style leaps that many other frogs make. Another difference is that most toads don't have teeth, whereas most other frogs do.

Frogs and toads live just about everywhere except in some extremely dry deserts, on some islands, and near the North and South Poles. More species live in wet tropical environments than anywhere else. For example, the country of Ecuador in South

Amazon river frogs live in northern South America. They reach 5 inches in length and have smooth skin and long legs. They're related to bullfrogs and leopard frogs in the United States.

Rococo toads from Argentina have 8-inch long fat, squat, and warty bodies.

America and the state of Colorado in the United States are about the same size. Ecuador has about 393 species of frogs. Colorado has 17. Costa Rica, in Central America, is about one-third the size of the state of Florida. Costa Rica has about 123 species of frogs. Florida has 23.

Some frogs and toads live on the ground. Others burrow underground, live in the water, or spend most of the time high in trees. Although most species are *nocturnal* (active at night), some are *diurnal* (active during the day).

Most frogs and toads are *oviparous* (they lay eggs). Generally they lay their eggs in water, and the eggs hatch into tadpoles. Toads lay their eggs in strings, like beads on a necklace. Some frogs lay their eggs in clumps. Others scatter them individually around the pond. At the start, tadpoles breathe through gills. Tadpoles that live in warm ponds, where there isn't much oxygen, soon begin to develop lungs. These tadpoles swim to the surface and gulp air. In contrast, water in cool mountain streams has plenty of oxygen. Tadpoles that live there don't develop their lungs until shortly before they transform into froglets.

Most tadpoles are fanatic little eating machines. Unless hiding from predators or sleeping, they eat constantly. Most are *herbivorous* (feeding on plants), and they eat a lot of algae. Some are *carnivorous* (eating animals); these eat insects, worms, and even other tadpoles, including those of their own species. Others are *omnivorous* (eating both plants and animals).

A tadpole doesn't suddenly wake up one day and find itself transformed into a frog. As it grows, a tadpole's body changes in many ways. The long, coiled intestine shortens into an adult-type gut, and a stomach develops. Moveable eyelids form. Skin glands mature. Legs develop—first the hind legs, then the front ones. Mouth parts change and a tongue develops. The bones harden. The tail shrinks to nothing, and the tadpole is now a frog. What started off as an algae-eating, swimming blob attached to a tail, ends up as a big-mouthed predator hopping or flopping about on four sturdy legs.

Instead of laying their eggs in the water, some frogs lay them inside fallen logs, in clumps of wet moss, in cavities in the ground, or in other moist sites where the eggs won't dry out. In some species the mother or father stays with the eggs and urinates on them to keep them moist. The parent also protects the eggs from

As a tadpole grows it goes through many changes, both inside and outside its body. Eventually it develops legs, its tail shrinks, and it becomes a frog.

predators. If the predator is a small insect or spider, the parent may simply eat it. If the intruder is another frog trying to eat the eggs, the parent may bite the intruder's head, block it from getting to the eggs, or wrestle to defend its young.

Some terrestrial eggs take a long time to develop, never pass through a tadpole stage, and finally hatch as miniature frogs. This is called *direct development.* Most frogs with direct development live in the wet tropical rain forests or cloud forests.

In other frogs that lay their eggs on land, the eggs hatch into tadpoles. In some of these, the tadpoles stay in their moist nests and develop without ever going into the water. They hatch with huge bellyfuls of yolk, and they grow by absorbing the yolk. They don't eat until after they metamorphose.

In certain other species, tadpoles that hatch away from water must get to water or they'll die. How can they do this? Glass frogs and leaf frogs lay their eggs on leaves hanging above the water. As they hatch, the tadpoles flip out of their jelly capsules and somersault into the water below. Female marsupial frogs carry their eggs in pouches on their backs. In some species, after the tadpoles hatch the mother dips into a puddle or pond. Using her hind feet, she pushes the tadpoles out of her pouch and into the water. Poison dart frogs lay their eggs on land. Depending on the species, either the mother or father watches over the eggs until they hatch. The tadpoles then slither up onto the back of the parent and ride piggyback until the parent shrugs them off into water.

Five species of frogs and toads don't lay eggs at all. Instead, they're *viviparous*—the young develop inside the mother and are born as miniature frogs. In three of these, the young feed on their own stores of yolk while developing. In the other two, the young feed on substances secreted from inside the mother's oviduct (the part of the mother's body where the young develop).

Adult frogs breathe through lungs and through their skin. The skin is so thin that oxygen can pass through and enter tiny blood vessels called capillaries. Red blood cells then carry the oxygen throughout the body. This system of breathing doesn't work well if the skin gets too dry. As long as a frog is in a moist environment, its skin glands produce enough mucus to keep the skin in good working order for breathing.

The diets of adult frogs are nearly as varied as the animals themselves. Almost all are carnivorous. Most eat any kind of insect, earthworm, or other *invertebrate* (animal without backbone) as long as it's the right size. Some species, however, are very picky and eat only certain types of food, such as ants and termites. Ant and termite-eating frogs often have small heads and narrow mouths that don't open very wide. In contrast, frogs with extra-large heads and wide mouths can grab hold of and eat large insects, other frogs, snakes, lizards, and even small birds and mammals. Most frogs capture their prey by flicking out their sticky tongues, slapping them onto the victims, and then flipping the tongues back into their mouths with lightning speed. The only two herbivorous frogs that we know about eat mushrooms and fruit.

Frogs protect themselves in many ways. Often the first line of defense is simply to avoid catching a predator's attention. Many species are cryptic or *camouflaged* (they blend in with their background). Brown toads squatting on mud, or green treefrogs perched in the bushes, are hard to see. Once a predator spies a frog, though, the frog might jump to escape. If the predator catches up, the frog might switch to one of its tricks. It might flip over and play dead. Who wants to eat a dead frog? It might bloat itself up by filling its lungs with air. Now the frog seems too big to eat. Or, it might ooze *poisonous* mucus from its skin glands.

Frogs range from tiny creatures hardly half an inch long to the Goliath frog from west-Central Africa, a giant that can reach almost 12 inches. Most species are somewhere in between these extremes, with body lengths of about 1 to 6 inches.

Why do you suppose this leaf frog has flipped onto its back and is playing dead? It's hoping to avoid being eaten.

ORDER URODELA: SALAMANDERS

The second largest order of amphibians is the Urodela, the tailed amphibians. At first glance salamanders resemble lizards, but if you look closely you won't see any scales. Instead, salamanders have moist skin, thanks to their mucous glands. Also, lizards have claws on their toes; salamanders don't. Almost all salamanders have four legs, although a few aquatic species have only two.

There are about 415 species of salamanders alive today. Most live in Europe, Asia, and North America. Some live in Central and South America, but there are none in Australia and only a few in far northern Africa. People in the United States often take salamanders for granted because in many areas they're common. In parts of the world, however, people have never seen—or heard of—salamanders.

Most salamanders live on the ground or in the water, but some climb trees and others burrow underground. Some of the most unusual-looking salamanders live in caves. Their skin is white, and their eyes are tiny and useless. They're skinny and their legs are spindly. Overall, they don't look very healthy. But they are. They're just adapted to a unique environment where there's no light.

Salamanders don't peep and squawk to communicate with each other. And they're rather nearsighted. They can't see another salamander unless it's close by. At close range, they communicate with each other by raising or flattening their bodies or by waving their tails. Salamanders also communicate by touch and smell.

Courtship among salamanders often involves physical contact. For example, the male may rub his chin glands against the female. These glands contain chemicals that encourage the female to mate. Males of some species are more aggressive. Rather than rub, they slap their chins against the females. Some even bite or scratch the females with their teeth and then rub their glands on the open areas. By doing this, the chemicals quickly enter the females' bloodstreams and they are overcome by desire.

Like frogs and toads, salamanders breathe in several different ways. Aquatic species generally breathe through gills, but some can also poke their snouts out of the water and breathe through their lungs. The lungs of aquatic salamanders serve a second function: They help the animals to stay at a certain depth. When there's a lot of air in its lungs, the salamander will float. If it wants to eat invertebrates from the bottom mud, the salamander exhales some of the air from its lungs and sinks. Aquatic salamanders also breathe

Salamanders live on land, in the trees, under the ground, and in the water. This one is aquatic.

through their skin. Most terrestrial salamanders breathe both through lungs and skin. One large family of salamanders, the Plethodontidae, lacks lungs. These "lungless salamanders" breathe only through their skin and the moist lining of their mouths.

Salamanders reproduce in various ways. Some lay eggs in the water and the eggs hatch into aquatic larvae that eventually metamorphose into the adult body form. Other species lay eggs on land. After a period of direct development, a miniature version of an adult salamander hatches. In many of the salamanders with direct development, the mother protects the eggs from drying out and defends them against predators. Four species of salamanders are viviparous. In two of these, the young feed on their yolk while inside the mother's body. Young of the other two species feed on substances secreted from the lining of the mother's oviduct.

Salamanders are carnivorous—both as larvae and adults. They eat a wide variety of insects, worms, snails, and tadpoles. Large salamanders with wide mouths can even eat fish, other salamanders, and small mice. Aquatic salamanders usually suck prey into their mouths. Terrestrial salamanders usually capture prey by slapping the prey with their large, sticky tongues and then jerking the tongues plus victims back into their mouths—much as frogs do.

Salamanders have many ways of protecting themselves against predators. If camouflage doesn't work, they try something else. Some species ooze poisonous secretions. Fire salamanders spray poison from their skin glands when they're attacked. They can even aim the spray at the predator. Some salamanders threaten predators by opening their mouths and lashing their tails. Sometimes the tail-lashing is more than a threat: The salamander oozes a sticky substance that works like glue on its attacker. Garter snakes that tangle with these salamanders sometimes can't free themselves from their own coils for a day or two!

Many salamanders can make their tails fall off when attacked by a predator, a behavior called *tail autotomy*. The tail keeps wiggling for a while after it breaks off, and the predator pounces on the tail while the rest of the salamander slinks off. In time a new tail will regenerate (grow back). Tail autotomy, however, costs the salamander something. First, regenerating a new tail takes a lot of energy that otherwise could be spent growing or reproducing. Secondly, the regenerated tail is usually smaller than the original one. The next time the salamander is attacked, the smaller tail might not divert the predator's attention as well.

The largest salamander in the world, the Japanese giant salamander, is also the largest living amphibian. Adults can reach over 5 feet and weigh nearly 90 pounds. The largest salamander in the United States is the hellbender, which can grow to 3 feet. Both of these large salamanders are aquatic. The largest terrestrial salamander is the tiger salamander, common in some parts of the United States. A big individual can reach 13 inches. In contrast, some lungless salamanders that live in Mexico are only about an inch long.

ORDER GYMNOPHIONA: CAECILIANS

The third group of amphibians is the legless caecilians. At first glance caecilians look like giant earthworms. Like earthworms, caecilians have annuli (rings) around their bodies. Their tiny eyes are usually covered by a thin layer of skin or bone. The tail is either short or absent. Caecilians have lungs, but in many species the left lung is small or absent.

Caecilians' skin always feels slimy because it's covered with mucus. In fact, it's hard to hold onto a squirming caecilian. Despite the slimy skin, however, caecilians have small scales beneath the surface of the skin. (Frogs and salamanders have no scales at all.)

About 165 species of caecilians live in the world's tropical regions: in Asia, Africa, and Central and South America. Most people in the United States have never seen or even heard of caecilians, because caecilians don't live here. Most species live underground, and even local people rarely see them. Some species are aquatic, and they're even harder to find. Although most caecilians are dull gray, brown, or black, some are blue, orange, pink, or bright yellow. Some are plain, others are striped.

Because of their secretive habits, we don't know much about caecilians. Our best guess is that about 70% of all caecilians are oviparous. In some aquatic species, the eggs hatch into larvae that develop in the water. Other species lay their eggs on land, the eggs have direct development, and the female stays with her eggs. Just as

Some caecilians live in the water. Others, such as this one from Thailand, burrow underground.

with frogs and salamanders, these mothers probably protect the eggs from predators and keep the eggs moist. About 30% of caecilians are viviparous. In these species, the young get nutrients from the mother while developing inside her body. They scrape the lining of the mother's oviduct with their teeth, and then feed on the secretions that ooze out.

Caecilians are unique: They are the only vertebrates that have tentacles. A caecilian has two tentacles, one on each side of the head, between the eye and the nostril. Because their eyes are fairly useless, caecilians use their tentacles for locating and identifying prey. They taste and smell with their tentacles. When they're not using them, they can withdraw their tentacles back into their heads.

Terrestrial caecilians often eat earthworms that wander into their burrows. Unlike a frog or a salamander, a caecilian doesn't use its tongue to capture prey. The caecilian slowly moves toward the worm until it can almost touch it, then it strikes and bites with its powerful jaws. The caecilian's long, fang-like, backward-curving teeth hold the worm secure. Aquatic caecilians eat a wide variety of invertebrates, including shrimp and insect larvae.

Caecilians can grow to 4 feet. They're slender, though, usually less than 1 inch wide. Many are no more than 10 inches long and less than half an inch wide. The smallest caecilians are only about 3 inches long as adults.

. . .

Aquatic or terrestrial, oviparous or viviparous, herbivorous or carnivorous, amphibians are fascinating animals. They're the transitional *vertebrates* between the fishes and the reptiles. Most scientists believe that amphibians evolved (changed over many, many years) from lobe-finned fishes. These ancient fishes had lungs and strong fins. During dry periods when their ponds dried up, lobe-finned fishes may have crawled about on land in search of water. Over millions of years, fins evolved into legs. Lungs became more efficient. Other changes evolved that allowed early amphibians to make better use of the land.

The earliest amphibian fossils date back to about 360 million years ago. These early amphibians were carnivores that grew to more than 3 feet in length. Amphibians were common in fresh water and on land for the next 70 million years. During this time some forms evolved into early reptiles. Some of the early reptiles eventually gave rise to the dinosaurs. By the time dinosaurs ruled the Earth, the number of amphibians had dwindled. Some persisted, however, and eventually evolved into the frogs, salamanders, and caecilians that we know today.

MEET THE REPTILES I

t's not very complimentary, but the word reptile comes from the Latin word *reptilis* meaning a creeping, crawling animal. There are 4 groups, or *orders,* in the class Reptilia. We'll look at two of these groups in this chapter. Turtles and tortoises belong to the Testudines (also called Chelonia). *Testudines* means a tortoise shell in Latin, and Chelonia comes from the Greek word *chelone* meaning tortoise. Turtles and tortoises are unique among reptiles: They carry their homes with them—their shells. Crocodilia, the crocodilians, includes crocodiles, gavials (also called gharials), alligators, and caimans. Crocodilia comes from the Latin word *crocodilus* meaning crocodile. These are the most prehistoric-looking of all the modern reptiles.

ORDER TESTUDINES: TURTLES AND TORTOISES

Turtles are perhaps the most easily recognized of all vertebrates because of their bony shells that provide instant protection. At the first hint of danger, a typical turtle draws its legs, tail, and head into the shell and shuts out the world. The top part of the shell is the *carapace* and the lower part is the *plastron*. These two parts are connected by a bony bridge on each side. In most turtles the shell is covered with sturdy *scutes* (plates made from *keratin*, the same hard material found in reptile scales and in your fingernails). In a few turtles, such as soft-shelled turtles and some sea turtles, the shell is covered with thick, leathery skin. Box turtles and most other turtles that live on land have high, dome-shaped carapaces. In contrast, painted turtles and most other aquatic turtles have flatter carapaces.

About 260 *species* of turtles share the planet with us today. Many live in the ocean and in fresh water, including rivers, streams, ponds, lakes, marshes, and swamps. Some live on land—in forests, deserts, and grasslands. Although most turtles are brown, black, or dull green, some have bright yellow, orange, or red spots or stripes. All turtles breathe with lungs. Some aquatic species also breathe underwater through the skin in their throat and hind end regions.

What's the difference between a turtle and a tortoise? Just as with poodles and dogs—and toads and frogs—all tortoises are turtles, but not all turtles are tortoises. Tortoises are certain turtles that live only on land. As you would expect, the feet of *aquatic* and *terrestrial* turtles are different. Many tortoises have stumpy hind feet, like elephants' feet. Gopher tortoises and Bolson tortoises use their front feet as scoops when they dig burrows in the sand. Freshwater turtles have webbed hind feet that allow them to swim efficiently. Sea turtles have flippers for feet, and they use these like oars to paddle through the water. Some sea turtles can swim as fast as our best Olympic swimmers!

Notice the high dome-shaped carapace on this baby tortoise from Argentina.

Turtles don't have teeth. Instead, their strong, razor-sharp jaws cut and crush their food. Some turtles slurp fish and small invertebrates from the water. Other aquatic turtles eat fruits and flowers that fall into the water. Snapping turtles eat just about anything they can swallow—fishes, frogs, snakes, snails, aquatic plants, and other turtles. Green sea turtles eat seaweed. Leatherback turtles eat jellyfish, composed mostly of water and stinging cells. Hawksbill sea turtles eat sponges, an amazing feat since the skeletons of sponges are made of silica (glass). Some tortoises are strictly *herbivorous* and eat only berries and other fruits, flowers, and leaves. *Omnivorous* tortoises eat both plants and animals such as insects, worms, and slugs.

Small turtles are food for crabs, fish, snakes, alligators, birds, and mammals. Killer whales and sharks eat large turtles. So, how does a turtle defend itself?

Some, such as box turtles and mud turtles, have hinges in their plastrons. After the turtle withdraws its head, feet, and tail into the shell, it can close the plastron tightly against the carapace. Have you ever tried to pry open a box turtle in this position? It's nearly impossible. Side-necked turtles don't have this option. The best they can do is bring their head and neck in alongside the body in the gap between the carapace and plastron—leaving them more vulnerable to predators.

The best defense for an aquatic turtle sunning itself on a log is to dive into the water and swim like crazy. Tortoises often bask at the entrances to their burrows. When they sense danger, they bolt down their tunnels and disappear from sight. Snapping turtles are aggressive and quick to bite with their strong jaws. Musk turtles are called "stinkpots" for good reason—a musk turtle gives off a foul-smelling substance from glands on its thighs when threatened.

Turtles communicate with each other primarily during courtship and aggressive interactions. For some species, vision is important. A turtle may bob its head up-and-down or side-to-side. Turtles sometimes open their mouths wide and threaten intruders. Many turtles use smell to determine whether another individual is a male or a female. Turtles also communicate by touch. A male might tap a female's head. Or he might rub her head. Sometimes male tortoises even make vocal sounds while following females during courtship.

All turtles, whether terrestrial or aquatic, lay their eggs on land. Typically, the female digs a hole in the ground, lays her eggs in the hole, and covers the eggs with dirt. In a few species, the mother doesn't bother making a nest. She simply lays her eggs on the surface of the ground, amidst fallen leaves. Turtles don't take care of their young. Instead, the sun's heat incubates the eggs. After the baby turtles break through their egg shells, they dig their way out of the ground to the surface.

The earliest turtles were around long before the dinosaurs. Their body form must have been a good one, because they haven't changed much in the past 200 million years. Turtles watched the dinosaurs go extinct, but they continued living.

Turtles are some of the world's longest-living vertebrates. Box turtles can live 50 years. Sea turtles and large tortoises can live as long as the average human. Tortoises can live to 100 years or more in captivity.

Leatherback sea turtles are the world's largest turtles. They can grow to 8 feet and weigh more than 1500 pounds. The largest tortoise is the Galápagos tortoise, which can reach 4 feet in length and weigh up to 600 pounds. Adults of some turtles, such as the common bog turtle, never get bigger than 4 inches.

ORDER CROCODILIA: CROCODILIANS

Crocodilians have short, strong legs, webbed hind feet, and long snouts. They breathe with lungs. Cone-shaped teeth fit into sockets in their strong jaws, just as our teeth do. Armor of bony plates covering their tough skin makes them look prehistoric. They use their powerful tails for swimming and as whips to defend themselves.

Most crocodilians live in the world's tropical and subtropical regions. Alligators, however, live a little farther north: in the southeastern United States and in China. Most crocodilians live in fresh water, but a few live in slightly salty or even sea water. Crocodilians are excellent swimmers. When they're not in a hurry, they often crawl on their bellies across land. Beware, though: Some can gallop surprisingly fast on land by lifting up their bellies high off the ground.

Scientists divide the 23 living species of crocodilians into 3 groups: (1) crocodiles, (2) gavials (also called gharials), and (3) alligators and caimans.

It's easy to tell crocodiles from the other 2 groups because the long, fourth tooth on each side of the lower jaw fits into a groove in the side of the upper jaw. When the crocodile's mouth is closed, these teeth are exposed. That's why crocodiles look fierce. Some of the 13 species of crocodiles live in salt water; others live in freshwater streams and rivers.

The 2 species of gavials have extremely long and slender snouts, with lots of sharp teeth exposed at the tip. The fourth tooth and all the teeth in front of it rest on the outside of the upper jaw when the mouth is tightly closed. When the mouth is open, even just a bit, all of the sharp teeth are exposed, giving this reptile a menacing look. Gavials live in freshwater rivers.

In alligators and caimans, the long fourth tooth on each side fits into a pit in the animal's upper jaw. When the mouth is closed you can't see the tooth, so alligators and caimans don't look as mean as other crocodilians. Another difference is that most crocodiles have pointed snouts, while alligators have rounded snouts. All 8 species of alligators and caimans live in or near fresh water.

Crocodilians engage in very active courtship. For example, male alligators bellow loudly and slap their heads against the surface of the water. All this commotion attracts females. A female places her snout on the male's head or snout, and the two rub each other's head and snout for awhile. Eventually, if the female is

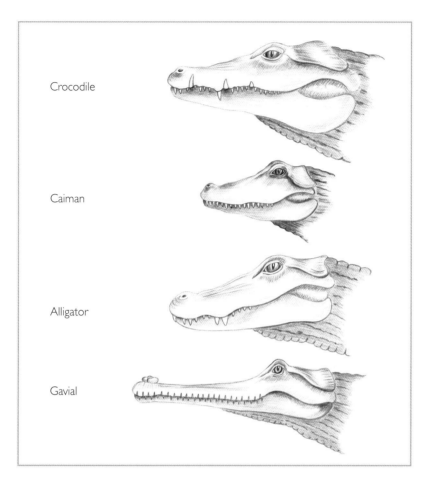

Crocodile

Caiman

Alligator

Gavial

What sharp teeth they all have! The crocodile, with its large fourth tooth exposed, looks the fiercest.

receptive, the animals circle each other in the water and blow bubbles. If the female is not receptive, she growls and swims away.

All crocodilians are *oviparous*. Alligators, caimans, and a few species of crocodiles lay their eggs inside nests that they build by heaping vegetation and soil into a mound. The heat from the sun and rotting vegetation incubates the eggs. Other crocodilians lay their eggs in nests they make by digging a hole in the ground. Female crocodilians guard their nests and are attentive mothers.

Parental care behavior of the American alligator is just as impressive as that of many birds. The young begin to peep even before they have completely emerged from their eggshells. Mom responds by ripping apart the nest. She gently nudges one or two babies into her mouth and then carries them to water. She repeats the process until all are safely swimming in their new home. Amazing—an animal whose jaws are strong enough to crush a human, carefully carrying its newly hatched babies in its mouth! Mom and her babies stay together for about two years, while she aggressively defends them against predators. Although the young are certainly

This American alligator appears to be snoozing on a lazy summer afternoon.

capable of finding their own food, they sometimes eat chunks of food that drop from their mother's mouth while she's eating. She doesn't mind . . . though you better believe she would fight any other alligator that tried to share her meal!

Crocodilians "talk" to each other. Babies peep while still inside their eggs, presumably communicating with each other. *Herpetologists* (scientists who study amphibians and reptiles) think this communication may enable the young to hatch at the same time. During the year or two that they stay near their mother, the young and Mom vocalize to each other as a way of keeping the family together. Whenever a young senses danger it peeps and Mom comes to the rescue. Even adult males vocalize. They bellow loudly during the breeding season, warning intruders not to enter their territories.

Young crocodilians eat insects and frogs. As they get bigger they eat fishes, turtles, birds, and mammals. Crocodilians usually feed at night, catching their prey in the water. A crocodilian lies in wait, floating in the water with just its eyes and nostrils above the surface. Spying dinner, it lunges and grabs the prey in its powerful jaws. If the catch is large, the crocodilian may drown it underwater before feeding. If a crocodilian captures an animal on land, it often drags the prey to water to eat it. It's probably easier for the crocodilian to eat while in the water.

A crocodilian doesn't chew its food. It tears the prey into bite-sized chunks and swallows those whole. If a catch is especially large, the crocodilian may wait to dine a day or more until the prey begins to rot. Then it's easier to tear apart. Crocodilians also swallow stones, which presumably help to grind and break up bones and other hard items in the stomach.

Many types of crocodilians shared the Earth with the dinosaurs. Some of these were huge. Fossil remains of one found in Texas include a skull nearly 6 feet long. If its body proportions were similar to those of our modern-day crocodilians, this giant could have been 45 feet long—as big as *Tyrannosaurus rex*, the meat-eating "King of the Dinosaurs." This huge crocodilian might have eaten small dinosaurs, perhaps even baby *T. rex*. Like the turtles, crocodilians watched the dinosaurs go extinct and they survived. They haven't changed much through the millions of years since.

The largest crocodilian, the saltwater crocodile, is also the largest living four-legged reptile. Some giants grow to 24 feet, more than half the length of *Tyrannosaurus rex*. Saltwater crocodiles live over a wide area, from India to northern Australia. People fear this species and the Nile crocodile because they're large and aggressive, and they'll eat humans if given the opportunity. The smallest crocodilians are dwarf caimans, usually less than 4 feet long. They live in small streams and pools in rain forests in the Amazon Basin. People swim with these caimans without fear because they're too small to eat humans.

MEET THE REPTILES II

The remaining two *orders* of reptiles are the largest and the smallest groups. The largest reptile order is Squamata, the lizards and snakes. Squamata comes from the Latin word *squamae* meaning scale. Even though they belong to the same order, we'll consider the lizards and snakes separately because these groups are so diverse. The smallest order is Rhynchocephalia, consisting of the two species of tuatara. Rhynchocephalia comes from the Greek words *rhynchos* and *kephale* meaning snout and head, in reference to the wide snout of these lizard-like reptiles.

ORDER SQUAMATA: LIZARDS

Both lizards and snakes belong to the order Squamata, largely based on similarities in their skeletons. So what's the difference between the two groups? You'll probably answer, "Of course, lizards have legs and snakes don't!" That's often, but not always, true. Some burrowing lizards don't have legs. For example, of the 133 species of worm lizards, only 3 have tiny legs; the rest have no legs at all. These lizards have long worm-like bodies, tiny eyes, and no external ears. Several other, unrelated lizards also burrow underground and lack legs.

Most lizards can blink their eyes, because they have moveable eyelids. Snakes lack moveable eyelids. Other differences between lizards and snakes involve organs and bones inside the body—structures you can't see.

The 3000 or so *species* of lizards come in an amazing diversity of shapes and sizes, from short and fat to long and skinny. Gila monsters and Mexican beaded lizards, the only two *venomous*

This thin tree iguana from Chile spends much of its time basking in the sun and eating insects. It will break off its long tail if you grab it by the tail!

lizards, are chunky with short, thick tails. In contrast, some slender legless lizards are nearly 50 inches long, two-thirds of which is tail. Skinks have smooth skin. Horned lizards and Australian thorny devils are spiny.

Lizards live almost everywhere in the world except in polar regions, although they're most common in warm areas. They live in hot deserts, lowland rain forests, wet cloud forests, high mountains, and everywhere in between. Regardless of where they live, all lizards breathe with lungs.

Lizards shed their skin from time to time, making room to grow larger. The worn-out skin usually comes off in large pieces, over several days. The new skin is often more brightly colored than the old skin that is about to be shed.

Most lizards are *oviparous*. In a few species, the female stays with her eggs until after they hatch. Some lizards bury their eggs in the sand, dirt, or under fallen leaves on the ground. Others wedge their eggs into crevices between rocks or hide them in rotting logs. About 20% of lizards are *viviparous*.

Lizard courtship often involves visual displays that are nearly as complex as those of birds. Males of many species have horns or crests that they show off when trying to attract females. During the breeding season, males of some species become brightly colored, and they display these patches of color to prospective mates.

Often males compete among themselves for opportunities to mate with females. In many species, males stake out territories that they defend from other males. The advantage in having a territory is that the owner can mate with any female that enters his area. Males defend their territories by using threatening body postures, bobbing their heads, and spreading out their *dewlaps* (throat fans).

Some males do push-ups and show their bright patches of color. If displays don't work, sometimes the lizards bite each other.

Lizards' diets are diverse. Many eat insects. Some eat scorpions. Marine iguanas dive up to 50 feet under the surface of the ocean to munch on seaweed. Young green iguanas eat insects, but as adults they prefer leaves, fruits, and flowers. Nile monitor lizards feast on crabs and crocodile eggs. Tokay geckos eat small mice and other lizards. Caiman lizards eat only snails, which they crush between their strong jaws.

Some lizards simply open their mouths, grab a prey with their jaws, and swallow it whole. Many, however, zap prey with their tongues. Chameleons are especially adept at this, and they're sometimes called the "sharpshooters of the lizard world." A chameleon's tongue can shoot out and latch on to an insect that's as far away as two chameleon body lengths (not counting the tail). Each of the chameleon's eyes swivels independently of the other. For example, the lizard can use one eye to scan for prey to its left and the other eye to scan straight ahead. When one eye spots a catch, the other swings around to focus on it as well. The depth perception (ability to judge distances) that both eyes now provide increases the chameleon's accuracy of zapping the prey.

Gila monsters and Mexican beaded lizards have venom glands in the tissue along their jaws. Unlike venomous snakes, these lizards don't inject the venom through fangs. Instead, the venom flows into the mouth. Then, when the lizard bites into a baby bird or other prey, the venom seeps into the puncture wounds.

These lizards also use their venom to protect themselves. If you ever see one of these reptiles, don't pick it up. If it gets a good hold of you and bites, its venom can be fatal. At the least, the bite will be painful, your blood pressure will drop, and you'll have trouble breathing. The venom of these two lizards is about as toxic to humans as cobra venom.

These venomous lizards are easy to recognize. Gila monsters are mottled and banded jet black and salmon pink. They're the largest lizards in the United States. Mexican beaded lizards are darker than Gila monsters, and they have white, cream, or pale yellow markings. Both of these lizards are good climbers, crawling high into trees in search of birds' nests. You will also find them on the ground, where they spend time in burrows.

Even for venomous lizards, often the best defense against predators is simply not to be noticed. Many lizards are *camouflaged*. Once they're noticed, the next defense may be running. Anoles run up trees. Chuckwallas run into crevices between rocks and take big gulps of air. By inflating their lungs, the lizards become larger and their bodies get tightly wedged in between the rocks, making it impossible for predators to get to them. A horned lizard makes a mad dash for the nearest clump of vegetation. Some desert lizards run a bit and then dive into the sand and disappear. A green iguana or an Asian water dragon basking on a tree branch overhanging a river will drop into the water below.

Once caught, a lizard will often defend itself. Those with strong jaws and sharp teeth bite. Those without weapons may bluff by hissing, squeaking, opening their mouths, or inflating their bodies. An Australian frilled lizard has a huge flap of loose skin around its neck that it spreads out when bothered—causing it to look much larger and fiercer than it really is. Some species startle their attackers. Horned lizards sometimes squirt blood from the corners of their eyes. Blue-tongued skinks flip out their bright blue tongues. Spinytail geckos spray a sticky substance from glands in their tails.

As a last resort, a lizard may drop its tail to save its life. When a predator grabs the lizard and the tail drops off, nerve reflexes keep the tail wiggling. If the lizard is lucky, the predator pounces on the tail while the lizard escapes. As in the case with salamanders, a new tail usually grows back, but often it's shorter than the original one and sometimes even a different color.

Lizards use their tails in other ways as well. Depending on the species, the tail may store fat, grasp onto tree branches, act as a balance while climbing in the trees, or serve to balance the lizard's body as it runs.

The largest lizards are the Komodo monitors, or Komodo dragons. Growing to 10 feet, these lizards live only on a few small islands in the Indonesian archipelago, including the island of Komodo. At the other extreme, some dwarf chameleons of Madagascar and Africa are only about an inch long. The smallest lizard is a newly discovered gecko, found on an island off the coast of the Dominican Republic. Its total length, including tail, is barely more than half an inch.

ORDER SQUAMATA: SNAKES

About 100 million years ago snakes evolved from lizard-like reptiles that had legs. Since then, snakes have lost their legs and developed different ways of moving. They've also lost the moveable eyelids that most lizards have. So, snakes can't blink their eyes. Instead, a transparent scale protects the eye.

How do all a snake's internal organs fit into its narrow, tube-like body? For starters, the left lung is either small or absent. Many of the other organs are displaced from their usual positions in other reptiles. For example, the kidneys are not across from each other. Instead one is located more forward than the other.

We have nearly 2700 species of snakes on Earth today. They live almost everywhere on the continents: in deserts, forests, grass-lands, oceans, and fresh water. Snakes are absent from most islands, however. More species of snakes live in the tropics than anywhere else. Snakes live on the ground, in crevices or burrows underground, in the trees, and in water. Like all other reptiles, snakes breathe with lungs. Sea snakes, however, also breathe underwater through their skin. Although most are harmless to humans, about 270 species of snakes have venoms that can harm or kill people.

Some naïve people assume that snakes all look alike. After all, they all have cylindrical bodies with no legs or wings to break up the shape. Those who study snakes, however, are impressed by their diverse appearances. Most snakes have long, slender bodies. A few, such as African puff adders, are heavy and robust. Sea snakes use their flattened tails as oars to paddle through the ocean. Many *arbo-real* (living in trees) snakes have huge, bulgy eyes. Burrowing snakes have tiny eyes and are nearly blind.

Some people think that snakes are slimy, but what they're feel-ing are hundreds of smooth, slippery scales. After all, snakes are reptiles, and reptiles have dry skin. Like lizards, snakes shed their skins. Instead of peeling off in large patches, however, a snake's skin usually comes off in one piece. Once the old skin begins to peel around the lips, a snake rubs the side of its head on the ground. This folds the skin back, and the snake crawls out of its old skin.

If you watch a snake closely, you'll see its narrow, forked tongue flicking in and out of its mouth. The snake is "tasting" its environment. Each time the tongue flicks out, it picks up chemicals. Flicking back in, the tongue touches the roof of the mouth and transfers the chemicals to a sense organ called the *Jacobson's organ*. This sense organ enables the snake to locate food and mates or to detect predators.

In fact, sensing chemicals by their tongues and Jacobson's organs is the main way that snakes communicate with others of the same species. Visual signals aren't used much, and because snakes don't have external ear openings they can't hear. They can pick up vibrations through whatever they're sitting on, however. Some snakes touch during courtship. The male may rub his chin against the female or even gently bite her.

All snakes are *carnivorous*. Among the foods of different snakes are ants, termites, grasshoppers, spiders, snails and slugs, centipedes, crayfish and crabs, fishes, frogs and caecilians, lizards, caiman, turtles, birds, mice and rats, deer, and the eggs of fishes, frogs, reptiles, and birds. Thus, it's not surprising that snakes capture and handle their prey in different ways.

Many snakes simply grab their prey with their jaws, work them into their mouths, and swallow. Boas and pythons coil around their prey and squeeze, or constrict, until the catch suffocates or its heart stops beating. Constriction allows a snake to tackle a large prey with less chance of getting hurt. For example, a large anaconda, 25 feet long, can constrict and eat a 6-foot crocodilian.

Another way to subdue a victim so that it can be eaten is to inject it with venom and wait for the animal to die. Substances in the venom begin to soften up the game, allowing the snake to digest

Rainbow boas, mostly shades of brown, orange, gray, and black, give off a blue iridescence in the sunlight.

its meal faster. Although venomous snakes can use their venom to protect themselves, it is mainly used to capture food.

Pit vipers, such as rattlesnakes, copperheads, and bushmasters, have pits located just above their mouths, one on each side, between the eye and the nostril. These pits are lined with heat-sensitive cells. A pit viper out cruising for a meal can sense heat coming from an animal that's warmer than the surroundings. This way of finding food works especially well for *endothermic* prey—birds and mammals. Have you ever looked closely at the head of a boa or python? Most boas and pythons also have heat-sensitive pits, just like the pit vipers. In boas and pythons, however, the pits are often located along the upper lip.

Snakes often eat game that are much wider than their heads. How does a snake with a 2-inch wide head swallow a large rat? The secret is that a snake's jaws are loosely connected, and the jaws can be separated into right and left halves. This is very different from a person's jawbone, which is solidly connected in the front. The two parts of the snake's lower jaw can move apart, allowing the snake to open its mouth wider. Once the prey is in its mouth, the snake moves its jaws sideways, first one side then the other until it works the animal down its throat. To understand how this works, imagine putting a pillow into a pillowcase that has shrunk and is a little too small. You would alternate pulling up one side of the pillowcase over the pillow, then the other, until the pillow was completely stuffed inside.

Some snakes are oviparous, others are viviparous. Even within one closely related group of snakes both forms of reproduction can occur. For example, boas and pythons both belong to the family Boidae. All pythons lay eggs, but all boas give birth to fully developed young. Some vipers, venomous snakes that belong to the family Viperidae, lay eggs; others are viviparous. For example, bushmasters, the largest vipers in the New World, are oviparous, whereas rattlesnakes are viviparous. Likewise, both oviparous and viviparous snakes occur in the family Elapidae, which includes the cobras, mambas, sea snakes, and coral snakes. There are differences even within the sea snakes. Most give birth to fully developed young at sea, but some slither onto land and lay eggs.

In some species of snakes, males fight among themselves in the presence of females. They coil around each other and each tries to pin the other to the ground. Usually the snake that stays on top of its opponent the longest wins. The winner mates with the female. Some snakes fight while lying on the ground. Others raise the front half of their bodies in a vertical position and duke it out, sometimes twisting their necks around each other. They sometimes sway their heads back and forth while facing each other, perhaps as a way of estimating the other's strength or size.

Snakes, like all other animals, have predators. To avoid them, many snakes blend in with their surroundings. When camouflage doesn't work and a snake has been detected, it usually tries to slither away quickly. Some snakes defecate when attacked. Dwarf boas squirt blood from their heads when harassed. If need be, the snake might bite the attacker—and some mean business with their venom.

The anaconda from South America and the reticulated python from Southeast Asia are the largest living snakes, growing to more than 25 feet. At 16 feet, the king cobra is the longest venomous snake in the world. Blindsnakes, some of the smallest snakes, measure only 6 inches as adults.

ORDER RHYNCHOCEPHALIA: TUATARA

Many people have never even heard of, much less seen, a tuatara. Although many species of tuatara lived on Earth 200 million years ago, only 2 exist today—on about 30 small islands off the coast of New Zealand. Both are considered *endangered* species. Tuatara look like lizards, but they're different from lizards in many ways, especially in their teeth and skulls.

Tuatara have crests of spines running down the centers of their backs. These crests are much larger in males than in females. In fact, the name tuatara comes from the Maori people native to New Zealand and means "spines on the back." The Maori do not add an "s" to the end of words to make the plural. So, although it seems natural to us to refer to tuataras, the plural is really tuatara.

Tuatara and various kinds of seabirds share their small islands. Both directly and indirectly, tuatara depend on the birds. These reptiles sometimes share burrows with the birds, or they take over burrows that ground-nesting birds have made and abandoned. Nesting seabirds are fairly messy, and they leave behind huge quantities of droppings, scraps of food, broken eggshells, and dead baby birds. This garbage attracts insects looking for food. Tuatara gather around these garbage heaps and eat the insects.

They'll even eat birds' eggs and baby birds when they get the chance. Baby birds are easiest to snag at night when they're asleep,

Tuatara resemble lizards, but they're not. They're the only living relatives of an ancient group of reptiles that were abundant during the time the dinosaurs ruled the Earth.

and insects gather around the garbage at night to feed. Thus, the tuatara do most of their feeding at dusk and dawn, rather than during the day when temperatures are warmer. Indeed, one unusual aspect about tuatara is that they're active at much cooler temperatures than are most other reptiles.

Tuatara are also unusual reptiles in that they really chew their food. In addition to insects, bird eggs, and baby birds, they eat earthworms, snails, and lizards. If the prey is small, a tuatara will capture it on its tongue, bring it into its mouth, and chew it until it's well-shredded. A tuatara impales larger meals on its large front teeth. After transferring the catch to the back of the mouth, the tuatara chews the animal thoroughly before swallowing it.

Tuatara communicate with each other mainly through visual signals. During courtship, a male becomes darker, elevates his spiny crest, raises the front half of his body high off the ground, and struts toward the female. A male defends his territory by elevating his crest and shaking his head from side to side at an intruding male. Usually the intruder flees, but if not, the territory owner opens his mouth wide and then quickly snaps it shut. Then he chases the intruder and may bite him.

Mating is a bit rough in tuatara, as the male sometimes gets carried away and bites the female. Ten to twelve months after mating, the female lays 8 to 15 eggs in her burrow. The eggs develop slowly for about 12 to 15 months before they hatch. This is the longest known incubation time for any reptile.

When they're not eating, tuatara spend much of their time in burrows, either ones they've dug or borrowed. During the day they bask in the sun at the burrow's entrance. Growth rate is very slow; tuatara don't reach maturity until they're about 20 years old. And they live a long time—some for over 70 years! Male tuatara can grow to 2 feet, and females are a little smaller.

* * *

And so we see why people have long been fascinated by reptiles. Their appearances and behaviors are not only intriguing, many are bizarre and amazing.

Though not as old as amphibians, reptiles go back a long way in time. The earliest fossil remains of reptiles are about 330 million years old. The period of time from about 245 million years to 65 million years ago is often called the Age of Reptiles because these animals were so diverse and abundant on Earth. Many of the early forms, including dinosaurs, went extinct. Fortunately, some of the others survived.

But how much longer will they be around? Many of today's reptiles and amphibians are threatened directly and indirectly by the activities of humans. Some species are declining in numbers. Others have gone extinct. The rest of this book is devoted to the causes of these declines and extinctions, and to the ways in which we can help protect these animals.

6

DISAPPEARING ACTS

*S*ilence of the Frogs. *Amphibians Out on a Limb. The Mystery of the Vanishing Frogs. The Case of the Disappearing Frogs. Frog Population Leaps Downward.* Articles with these titles have appeared in newspapers and magazines over the past dozen years. What's happening? Recently, several *species* and *populations* of amphibians have gone extinct. But before going further, we need a more complete definition of a species and a population.

A species consists of all the individuals that could breed successfully with one another if they were all in the same place, but could not breed with individuals of other species. For example, green treefrogs in a pond in Florida could breed with green treefrogs in North Carolina, if only they could get together, but they could not breed with squirrel treefrogs in the same pond. The green treefrogs in the Florida and North Carolina ponds belong to one species, but to different populations.

A population, then, consists of individuals of a species that actually *do* live together and have the opportunity to mate with one another. A species may consist of many different populations each separated from one another, or of only one population.

In the United States, populations of western toads have declined or disappeared from the Rocky Mountains, the Sierra Nevada Mountains, and the Cascade Mountains. Many populations of red-legged frogs have disappeared from California and Oregon. Populations of cricket frogs have declined or disappeared from the Midwest. All over the country, from New York and New Jersey to California, populations of tiger salamanders have declined or disappeared. Ditto for populations of southern dusky salamanders from South Carolina and Florida. These are just a few examples of many from throughout the world.

So many amphibians around the world seemed to be in trouble by 1990 that *herpetologists* met to discuss the problem. The scientists vowed to survey more areas to determine the extent of amphibian declines, investigate the possible causes, and educate the public about the problem. Since then, we've spent a lot of time, energy, and money on these three goals.

We've found that some amphibians are declining on all continents, from high in the mountains to low deserts and rain forests. In some cases the cause is obvious. Cutting down a rain forest and converting it to pasture for cattle destroys homes for amphibians. A fungus that attacks frogs' skin has wiped out some amphibian populations. This fungus has killed frogs in the United States, Central and South America, Africa, Australia and New Zealand, and Europe. Hardest hit seems to be Australia. By 2002, the fungus had affected 46 species of frogs from Australia (20% of the total number of frog species on the continent). Other documented causes of population declines include pollution, overexploitation, severe weather, and introduced species. In some cases, the cause of a particular population decline is still a mystery. Newspaper articles, magazine stories, and radio and television reports about declining and disappearing amphibians appear frequently and inform the public about the problem.

My personal experience with amphibian declines is the Costa Rican golden toad, one of the world's most spectacular toads. Males were brilliant golden-orange. Females had black, yellow, and scarlet-red spots. Apparently only one population of the golden toad existed, and this was in the Tilarán Mountains in north-central Costa Rica. In 1987 I studied over 1500 toads there. The next year I found only 1. My graduate student, Frank Hensley, saw the last golden toad in 1989. What happened to them? The wet, lush forest where the toads lived, the Monteverde Cloud Forest Reserve, is protected from habitat disturbance and from collectors. The toads should have been safe there. The year 1986–1987, though, was unusually warm and dry. Quite possibly the toads dried up and died.

Disappearance of an amphibian population isn't all that unusual because these animals are sensitive to changes in the weather. The problem for the golden toads was that apparently this was the last population left. Perhaps in the past other populations of golden toads lived in nearby mountains, disappearing one by one due to various causes until there was just the one left in the Monteverde reserve. Now it appears that the last population has disappeared.

Gastric brooding frogs from Australia have also disappeared. One species was discovered in 1973 but hasn't been seen since 1981.

Discovered in 1984, the second species was last seen the following year. These frogs were unique. In both species, the female swallowed her eggs (up to 24) and then brooded the tadpoles in her stomach. After the tadpoles metamorphosed into miniature frogs, the mother belched them back up. These were the only animals in the world known to brood their young in their stomachs. Scientists discovered that the tadpoles released a substance that stopped the mother's stomach from producing digestive acids—thus preventing her from digesting her babies. While the tadpoles were in their incubator, the mother simply didn't eat. This period of time lasted at least 8 weeks! After the froglets left, her stomach produced acids again and she could eat. Medical researchers had planned to study these frogs. They hoped that gastric brooding frogs could teach us something about shutting down production of digestive acids, perhaps leading to remedies for stomach ulcers in humans. By the time the researchers had planned their studies, though, the frogs had disappeared.

In some places, many amphibians seem to be in trouble at once. In the Yosemite area of California at least 5 species of frogs and toads that used to be common in the early 1900s are now hard to find. In certain areas of Australia, numerous species are declining or disappearing. In these and other cases of many species going downhill at once, scientists worry that something serious is wrong with the local environment, but it's hard to say just what that is.

In fact, many scientists suggest that amphibians may be good indicators of the general health of the environment. Their global decline may signal environmental deterioration that eventually may affect other organisms as well. Amphibians may be like the canaries that coal miners used as early warning systems in the mine shafts.

Poisonous gases frequently collected in the shafts and made the air unsafe for the miners to breathe. They took caged canaries down with them because the birds were more sensitive to the fumes than the miners were. As long as the canaries remained alive, the miners knew the air was safe for them. If the canaries died, the miners quickly evacuated.

• • •

While amphibians are getting a lot of attention right now, it's important to realize that reptiles are declining and disappearing too. In fact, many scientists believe that snakes are disappearing faster than any other group of *vertebrates*. At least 21 species of reptiles have gone extinct since 1600. Of these, 20 species lived only on islands. These extinct reptiles include tortoises, geckos, iguanids and other lizards, and burrowing boas and several other snakes.

The Galápagos Islands sit on the equator, in the Pacific Ocean 600 miles west of the coast of Ecuador. Beginning in the 1500s, whalers, buccaneers, and explorers who visited these islands severely reduced or wiped out entire populations of giant Galápagos tortoises. Sailors commonly loaded up to 400 tortoises at a time onto their ships. Because the tortoises could be kept alive for a long time, the sailors could have fresh meat for many months. In total, they took more than an estimated 100,000 tortoises for food.

Several kinds of iguana lizards have completely disappeared from some of the South Pacific islands where house cats have been introduced. Goats and pigs that people have brought onto the islands destroy so much of the vegetation, both by eating and by trampling it, that the lizards have a hard time hiding from the cats.

The Chinese find turtle and tortoise meat to be irresistibly delicious. They've eaten so many turtles from their own country that it's hard to find turtles there anymore. Now the Chinese import turtles from Bangladesh, Pakistan, India, and Nepal. Each year in China an estimated 12 million turtles and tortoises are sold for their meat. Herpetologists fear that soon many species of turtles and tortoises from Southeast Asia will be gone forever.

Many populations of boas and pythons are also dwindling. Millions of these animals are killed and made into belts, purses, wallets, and shoes. Although many species are currently protected, they are still hunted and people buy these articles illegally. Some species of crocodilians are becoming rare because their skins also make lovely belts, purses, wallets, and shoes. Human greed may exterminate some of these reptiles within this century.

• • •

Why might some amphibians and reptiles decline or go extinct while others survive quite well? The following features may help to answer this question.

COMPLEX LIFE CYCLES

Most amphibians have complex life cycles, meaning they pass through a distinct change in body shape. They metamorphose. Complex life cycles often involve change in habitat, and in the case of amphibians this change is usually from water to land. They're exposed to double jeopardy—if there's a problem with either environment they might not survive. A population of toads that lays eggs in a polluted pond will not survive long even if the woods are still a perfect home for the adults.

HIGHLY PERMEABLE SKIN

Amphibians have highly *permeable skin*, which means that substances can enter and pass back out through the skin easily. This is both an advantage and a disadvantage. The advantage is that amphibians can absorb water through their skin just by sitting on wet leaves or mud. The disadvantage is that water passes back out, too, so amphibians dry out easily. If the climate changes and becomes drier, they may die. Another disadvantage is that toxic chemicals from the air, water, and soil can easily enter their bodies and poison them. It's partially because of their highly permeable skin that amphibians may be good indicators of the state of health of the environment.

LARGE BODY SIZE

People's activities often affect large animals more than small ones. Large animals tend to have lower *population densities* (number of individuals in a given area) than small animals. If hunters go into an area and kill 50 large boas for their skins, the population is more likely to go extinct than if collectors remove 50 small wormsnakes from the same area to sell as pets, as there were probably many more wormsnakes to begin with.

LONG LIVES

Many reptiles live for a long time. Some snakes live for over 20 years, and some turtles and tortoises live for 50 to 80 years or even longer. Some crocodilians and tuatara live for over 70 years. The problem is that these long-lived reptiles don't reproduce very quickly. Many of them take a long time to reach reproductive maturity, and then they only breed every 2 to 4 years. In order to reach the age when they can reproduce, these reptiles must survive not only many years of predators, but also many years of environmental and human-caused threats.

POOR DISPERSAL ABILITIES

Some amphibians, especially small salamanders, don't move around much. For example, red-backed salamanders often move less than 2 feet in a day. They don't even move around much within their life-times. What would happen if their habitat were polluted or con-verted to a parking lot? The salamanders wouldn't be able to disperse (move away) far enough to find suitable habitat elsewhere and they'd die.

RESTRICTED DISTRIBUTION ON CONTINENTS

Many reptiles and amphibians live only in a particular area or region. Imagine a frog species that lives only in streams on one mountain, at an elevation of 3500 feet. It tolerates only a narrow range of temperatures, and it feeds only on the insects found in those streams. A mining company pollutes the streams and all the frogs die. Because there was only one population, the species has now gone extinct.

ISLAND POPULATIONS

Species that live on islands often have few natural predators, and over time they lose the ability to deal with them. Therefore, island species are especially vulnerable to introduced predators such as house cats.

COLONIAL NESTING HABITS

Reptiles that gather in large groups to lay their eggs are called *colonial nesters*. In some sea turtles, over just a few days, thousands of females clamber out of the ocean and drag themselves onto the beach to lay their eggs. All this activity attracts predators. Raccoons and dogs dig up the eggs and eat them. People, even more efficient than dogs and raccoons, dig up the eggs by the thousands and sell them for food because sea turtle eggs are considered a delicacy almost everywhere in the world where they're available.

MIGRATORY BEHAVIOR

Animals that migrate long distances have their own set of problems. Even if a species is protected in one country, it may not be protected in other countries. Green sea turtles are protected in Australia, but when they migrate to Indonesia people kill them for their meat and collect their eggs. Any species that migrates is potentially exposed to a wider range of threats than a species that stays in one place. A migratory species might have to swim through polluted waters or travel through forests disturbed by humans. Even animals that migrate less than a mile to breeding sites might need to cross highways and risk being squashed under the tires of vehicles.

7

WHY SHOULD WE CARE?

Some people ask, "Why should I care if amphibians and reptiles disappear? Extinction is a natural process, isn't it?" That's a worthwhile question. Extinctions have occurred ever since the beginning of life on Earth. *Species* form and then die out naturally. These are called natural extinctions. Scientists estimate that over 99% of all plant and animal life that ever existed on Earth has gone extinct.

Everyone knows about dinosaurs, but no human being has ever seen one alive. The last dinosaurs died out about 65 to 70 million years ago. They weren't the only animals to go extinct about this time, though. Along with them went the large flying reptiles, the swimming reptiles, and many smaller animals. This was a mass extinction. Some scientists believe that these extinctions were gradual, happening over millions of years. One theory is that perhaps the dinosaurs and other animals couldn't cope with changes in the weather that were caused by a large asteroid that crashed into the Earth in what is now the Gulf of Mexico.

Extinctions happening now are different. Scientists estimate that current extinctions occur at a rate at least 1000 times faster than most that happened in the distant past. Most current extinctions are caused either directly or indirectly by humans. Some experts believe that an average of at least one species of plant or animal disappears each day.

Many thousands of plants and animals will go extinct within your lifetime. Some of the animals will be amphibians and reptiles. In most cases these won't be natural extinctions. Instead, they'll happen because people are taking those animals' homes, their food, and their lives. We should care about present-day extinctions because we are the cause of most of them. Too many of us put too many demands on the environment. Present-day extinctions are also different from past ones because many can still be prevented. Humans may be the problem, but we can also be the solution. That's why we should care.

From a scientist's point of view, we should care about the disappearance of amphibians and reptiles because we're still learning about these animals—what they eat, how they defend themselves against predators, how they take care of their young, and how they cope with changing environments. Every year we discover new species, especially from areas of the world that haven't been thoroughly explored. Amphibians and reptiles are fascinating, and we should want them around so that we can learn more about them.

A somewhat selfish reason we should care about the health of amphibian and reptile *populations* is that we use these animals for our benefit: medical research, food, and leather. Many people also keep amphibians and reptiles as pets. These animals serve as an important source of inspiration for people all over the world, in religion and in folklore. When we lose amphibians and reptiles, we lose part of our culture.

Perhaps the most important reason we should care is that all plants and animals (including humans) are linked together in a "chain of life." When one species dies out, other species are affected. Why? Animals and plants serve as food and provide shelter for other organisms. Animals are major predators on other species. Without predators, the prey species would become so abundant that individuals wouldn't find enough food—and their populations would crash. Insects, birds, and bats inadvertently carry pollen from one plant to another and thus pollinate the plants. Without the animals, these plants would go extinct. Birds and mammals eat fruits and disperse the seeds. Without the animals, these plants would disappear. Plants rely heavily on animal droppings for nutrients.

What might happen if there were no frogs left to eat mosquitoes and other disease-carrying insects? Many more people in tropical countries would die from malaria and other diseases. If there were no frogs left to eat insects that damage our crops, we'd be in big trouble. In fact, this happened in India. So many frogs were collected so their legs could be sold to restaurants that in areas where the frogs were hunted, insect pests destroyed huge quantities of crops. Since 1987 India has banned the export of frog legs. The country now appreciates the value of frogs and wants to keep them around.

What if we had no snakes left to eat little furry pests? Again, we'd be in trouble, and it could happen in some places. In the spring, more than 50 towns in Oklahoma, Kansas, Texas, Georgia, New Mexico, Alabama, and Pennsylvania hold "rattlesnake round-ups." Rattlesnakes are collected and thrown into pits. Visitors can buy live snakes, dried and mounted snakes, snake meat, snake skins, snake heads and rattles made into cheap souvenirs, fat for making snake oil, and gall bladders for Oriental folk medicines. In Oklahoma alone, hunters collect an estimated 10,000 diamondback rattlers for roundups each year. A rattlesnake eats hundreds of rats, mice, and rabbits in its lifetime. So, when hunters remove thousands of snakes from the countryside, rats, mice, and rabbits multiply in large numbers. Rabbits eat farmers' crops. Rats and mice eat grain and spread disease. Thus, each rattlesnake is valuable to a farmer. Without the snakes to eat these pests, farmers must rely more on pesticides that are both expensive and toxic to the environment.

You might not think that tadpoles are as important as tigers, or rattlesnakes as important as rhinoceroses. The role an animal plays, though, doesn't depend on its size—or how cute and fuzzy it is. All of nature is worth conserving because each animal is an important link in the chain of life.

What do we mean by conserving nature? The word conserve comes from two Latin words—*servare,* meaning to guard or keep safe, and *con,* meaning together. *Conservation* is the protection and careful use of a natural area, plant, animal, or other natural resource to make sure it's still around far into the future.

8

WE'RE TAKING TOO MANY

One reason that some amphibians and reptiles are declining or disappearing is that people are simply collecting too many of them. Unfortunately for them, these animals have beautiful skins, are good to eat, make interesting and exotic pets, are ingredients in folk and modern medicines, or are useful in teaching and research.

International buying and selling of amphibians and reptiles is big business. The value of these animals and their products imported into the United States every year is hundreds of millions of dollars. Live animals, mostly for the pet trade, account for a small part of this. Most of the money is in products: frog legs for human consumption, and skins and manufactured items such as shoes, boots, and purses.

SKINS AND SOUVENIRS
Not all leather comes from cows. Believe it or not, people use frog

skin to make shoes, purses, belts, and key cases, and for binding small books. Frog skin makes an appealing covering for artificial fishing bait—or at least fish seem to think so. Toad skins make unusual change purses and shoes. Crocodilian leather is expensive: $600–$800 for a pair of shoes, $300 for a belt, and $1500–$3000 for a purse. You can even buy buttons covered with reptile skin.

Many *species* of boas, pythons, crocodilians, and lizards are currently declining because they're heavily hunted for their skins. Boa constrictor and reticulated python skins are made into shoes. The skins of tegu lizards, large terrestrial lizards that can reach 2 to 3 feet in length including the tail, are made into cowboy boots. The numbers of reptile skins bought and sold each year vary depending

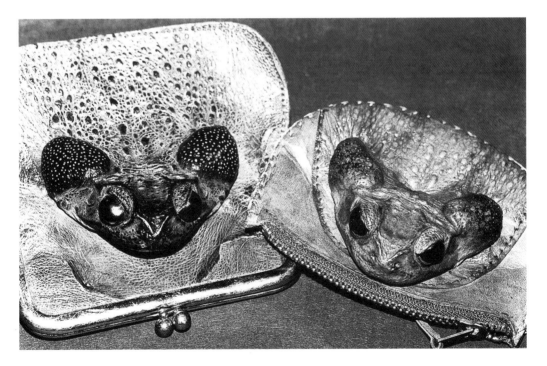

Two marine toads were killed to make these unusual change purses. Would you buy them?

on supply and demand, but on average the reported number is about 10 million skins sold by one country and bought by another. Just imagine what this figure would be if we added all the smuggled skins! The main countries that sell reptile skins are Indonesia, Singapore, Thailand, and Argentina. The main countries that buy the skins (to make into shoes and other articles) are Singapore, the United States, Italy, and Spain.

Have you seen combs and eyeglass frames that are mottled brown, yellow, black, and reddish-brown? They're called "tortoiseshell," but most are plastic. Real tortoiseshell comes from the *scutes* of hawksbill sea turtles, not tortoises. These scutes have beautiful patterns of amber, reddish-brown, blackish-brown, and yellow. In the eighth century, the Japanese began carving turtle shells into jewelry and combs, recently adding shoehorns and eyeglass frames. Until the early 1600s the crafts were made almost exclusively for the upper class of people. They are still considered a luxury.

Many amphibians and reptiles, or their body parts, are made into cheap souvenirs. Rattlesnake rattles and crocodilian teeth, claws, and feet are made into key chains. Even the heads of hatchling crocodilians are made into key chains. Toads, iguanas, and turtles are stuffed with cotton, fitted with glass eyes, and varnished to make their skins shine. In Mexico, Central America, and South America, stuffed toads playing billiards or musical instruments are sold in tourist shops.

FOOD

If you needed to hunt to feed yourself, how would you decide which animals to hunt? You would probably want the animals to taste good, be fairly easy to catch, and provide a good source of protein. Unfortunately for many species of amphibians and reptiles, they meet all 3 of these requirements.

People who hunt just to feed themselves or their families usually don't kill many animals. Commercial hunters, though, slaughter huge numbers of animals to sell for profit. Most of these animals are shipped to cities or foreign countries where they're made into gourmet dishes such as stir-fried frog legs smothered with oyster sauce, frog legs teriyaki, giant bullfrog chop suey, stuffed alligator steaks, poached alligator tail, turtle goulash, iguana stew, and fried, barbecued, or baked rattlesnake.

Frog legs are especially popular. With a body length of 7 to 8 inches, a bullfrog has BIG, muscular legs! During the first half of the twentieth century, so many people craved frog legs, and the prices were so high, that hunters in Florida earned up to $500 per day catching frogs. Now we import many of the frog legs eaten in the United States, up to 2000 tons each year. In France, 3000 to 4000 tons of frog legs are eaten each year. Most frog legs are imported from Indonesia and Bangladesh. Asia exports about 200 million pairs of frog legs each year, mostly to the United States, Europe, and Australia.

Central Americans have eaten green iguanas and spiny-tailed iguanas for centuries. Professional iguana hunters capture large numbers of the lizards and ship them to cities. People eat them not only because they taste good (like chicken), but also because they believe the lizards will improve their health. Eggs that are still in the body of the female are considered a delicacy.

Over half of Asia's freshwater turtles are heavily hunted for food and are in danger of extinction. The meat, said to be delicious, is considered to be a luxury food, often six times more expensive than chicken or lamb. To impress guests, turtle is the meat of choice.

Recently, people have killed large numbers of water snakes in Cambodia because the fish harvest wasn't as good as usual. During the peak of the 1999–2000 wet season, Cambodians harvested and sold an average of 8500 water snakes every day. People bought the meat for themselves as an inexpensive substitute for fish. They also fed them to crocodiles they were raising for sale. This is probably the largest harvest of any species of snake in the world.

PETS

Amphibians and reptiles are popular as pets—especially the bizarre, exotic, and brilliantly-colored ones. In fact, just within the United States, over 8 million amphibians and reptiles are currently kept as pets. Some of the more popular ones include the large-mouthed pac-man frogs; purple, blue, red, green, or yellow poison dart frogs; big-eyed geckos; colorful chameleons; green iguanas; massive boas and pythons; and, of course, charming box turtles and small tortoises.

International trade of live amphibians and reptiles for pets is a big business. In addition, there's a huge black market trade supplied by smugglers. Following are examples of the numbers of animals that were collected from the wild during 1990–1994 to be sold as pets. And these are just the numbers we know about:

- Tortoises   214,924
- Monitor lizards   228,091
- Chameleons   278,413
- Boas and pythons   652,124
- Poison dart frogs   20,962

By the late 1990s the international trade in live reptiles was growing. For example, in 1998 over 65,000 live reptiles were exported from Tanzania—mostly spinytailed lizards, geckos, and chameleons destined for the pet market. This is about 10 times as many live reptiles as the country exported in 1991.

The United States is the world's largest buyer and seller of live reptiles. Approximately 2.5 million live reptiles have been imported into the country each year since the late 1990s. Nearly half of these are green iguanas, one of the most popular reptile pets. Fortunately, most of these animals are born in captivity, rather than caught in the wild. In 1996, the United States exported about 9.5 million live reptiles, mainly to Europe and eastern Asia—both for the pet trade and the food market. Nearly 90% of these animals were red-eared slider turtles, born in captivity. All of these numbers are just to impress upon you just how huge the pet trade is!

As with many situations, the pet trade has two sides. On the one hand, more people interested in amphibians and reptiles means that more people will be willing to help conserve these animals and protect their habitats. On the other hand, each year many hundreds of thousands of amphibians and reptiles are collected in foreign countries and shipped to pet stores, mostly in the United States and Europe. Many of these die before they make it to their destination.

Those that do arrive alive rarely survive even six months in captivity because their new owners don't know how to care for their pets.

Even within the United States many animals are collected for the pet trade. In 1990, the Florida Game and Fresh Water Fish Commission started gathering information on the number of amphibians and reptiles collected in the state and sold. Everyone who collects and sells these animals must report on their collecting activities. The first two years' worth of data (1990–1992) are astounding: Nearly 120,000 amphibians and reptiles were collected in Florida. (No doubt many more animals were collected but not reported.) Of these, nearly 50,000 were snakes and nearly 42,000 were frogs and toads. That's a lot of animals for one state! The most popular species collected during these two years were corn snakes (13,827 individuals) and green treefrogs (13,166 individuals). How many years can *populations* of corn snakes and green treefrogs withstand this level of collecting?

FOLK AND MODERN MEDICINE

People all over the world use amphibians and reptiles to make folk medicines hoping to cure toothache, rheumatism, heart disease, kidney problems, ulcers, and even cancer. Iranians drink broths made from snakes (especially vipers) and tortoises to fight diseases. Jelly made from freshwater turtle shells is widely used in traditional Chinese medicine to improve general health. The jelly is also believed to cure cancer. Taiwan currently imports over a hundred tons of turtle shells per year to make traditional medicines.

Many people believe that reptile fat has medicinal properties. In Asia, people use fat from monitor lizards as a salve for bacterial skin infections. In Central America, fat from iguana lizards is used to heal burns and cuts. Crocodilian fat is used to cure asthma in the Dominican Republic and in Haiti. People in Madagascar use crocodilian fat to treat burns and ulcers of the skin.

Not only cultures outside the United States use amphibians and reptiles in folk medicine. There are plenty of old remedies from this country as well:

- To cure a toothache, roast 100 frogs in the oven. Make a powder of the dried bodies and then mix the powder with salt. Rub the mixture on your gums.

- To stop bleeding, put a pile of frog eggs on the wound and let the eggs dry.

- To heal an open sore, fry a frog in fat. Cover the sore with the liquid from the pan.

- To get rid of a wart, cut off the head of a turtle and put some of the blood on the wart.

- To protect yourself from harm, wear a string of rattlesnake vertebrae around your neck.

- To cure and prevent headache, wear a rattlesnake's rattles in the lining of your hat.

People from many different cultures use secretions from toads as medicines. When a toad is disturbed, it may defend itself by secreting a white fluid from large *parotoid* glands on its head. This secretion tastes bad to a would-be predator and may be irritating or *poisonous* as well. Eighteenth-century physicians used powder made from dried toads to lower a person's fever. The Chinese make a powder from toad secretions. Called *Ch'an Su,* the powder is mixed with flour and other ingredients and formed into cakes. It's used in treating heart ailments, for drying boils and abscesses, and for healing ulcers. Indian healers in Veracruz, Mexico, make medicines from toad secretions that supposedly also function as "love magic."

It seems odd that toad secretions are so widely used as medicine. The reason? It turns out they contain chemicals known to stimulate the human heart and to help the human body deal with stress. Don't you wonder how people in these different cultures figured this out independently?

Capsules containing the powder from dried rattlesnake skin, flesh, and ground-up bone are a common folk remedy in parts of the southwestern United States and Mexico. The powder supposedly cures various ailments ranging from skin and kidney diseases to cancer.

Amphibians and reptiles are used in modern medicine also. If you ever get bitten by a *venomous* snake, you may be rushed to the hospital to get a shot of *antivenin,* a substance that counteracts the snake's venom. Antivenin is made in a series of stages. First, venom is extracted from venomous snakes. Next, the venom is injected into a horse or sheep over and over, but not so much that it kills the animal, until the horse or sheep develops immunity to the venom. At this point the animal's blood contains antibodies, special proteins that destroy the venom. Blood is then drawn from the horse or sheep, and the serum containing the antibodies is purified in a laboratory. When this serum is injected into someone who has been bitten by a venomous snake, the person has a good chance of surviving—thanks to the antibodies produced by the horse or sheep. Venom extraction facilities around the world produce antivenins to save people's lives from snakebite.

With skill and caution, a technician "milks" venom from a fer-de-lance (a pit viper) in a venom extraction institute in Costa Rica. *Photo by Peter Feinsinger*

Because frogs live in wet environments, they are constantly exposed to bacteria and fungi. Some species of frogs have chemicals in their mucous secretions that protect them from infection. Can these chemicals be of medical use for humans? An antibiotic cream recently made from the skin secretions of African clawed frogs is meant to treat skin ulcers in people who have diabetes. Once this cream has been officially approved by the FDA (U. S. Food and Drug Administration), it will be extremely valuable. The reason is that the antibiotics we currently use don't always kill the disease organisms found in the ulcers.

RESEARCH AND TEACHING

Amphibians and reptiles themselves, not just their chemicals, are in great demand for medical and biological research. We even send frog eggs to outer space to learn about the effects that weightlessness might have on development. Amphibians and reptiles are also widely used in teaching, for dissections and demonstrations.

Researchers and teachers generally buy the animals from biological supply houses, which buy the animals from people who make a living by collecting them in the wild. Unfortunately, collectors rarely are concerned about the future of wild populations. They're out to make a profit and they wipe out populations by capturing every animal possible. And then the collectors move elsewhere. Each year, tons of frogs are collected from the wild for research and teaching purposes.

9

WE KILL THEM INDIRECTLY, TOO

Amphibians and reptiles suffer from human presence in ways other than being killed for food, handbags, or medicines. The things we do often affect these animals even if we have no intention of harming them.

We modify or destroy their habitat. Animals that we introduce into areas where they don't occur naturally sometimes eat the local amphibians and reptiles, destroy the habitat, or compete for the same food. We also contaminate the environment with toxic chemicals, indirectly killing amphibians and reptiles.

HABITAT MODIFICATION AND DESTRUCTION

Ecologists and *conservation* biologists agree that the most fundamental threat to the environment is the growing human *population*. Our worldwide population in 2001 was more than 6 billion. It's expected to reach 9.4 billion by the year 2050.

This means an average increase of 7,683 people per hour, or over 67 million more people in the world per year. The more people there are, the greater demand there is on the land. Each year the human race needs more land to support the extra people who weren't here the year before. More and more forests and open spaces that used to be home for amphibians and reptiles are being destroyed and converted to crop fields, shopping malls, and residential areas— places for humans to raise food, buy and sell goods, and live.

During the 1990s, about 80 acres of forest around the world were cut down every minute. That amounts to about 45 million acres every year. It's hard to envision 45 million acres, but it's about the size of the states of Florida and Maryland combined. And that's every year!

Only between 2% and 5% of the original, uncut forest remains in the United States. The rest has been logged or disturbed in some way by humans. We cut down forests and convert the land to fields of corn, potatoes, wheat, or other crops. We used to leave wetlands (swamps and other wet areas) for the frogs, salamanders, turtles, water snakes, and alligators because we thought these areas were unsuitable for human habitat. Now we drain out the water, fill the areas with sand, and transform them into golf courses and shopping malls. Over the past 200 years, an estimated 120 million acres of wetland in the United States have disappeared—a little more than half what we had in the late 1700s. Only recently have we realized that wetlands are not wastelands. They're a valuable and critical part of the landscape for many types of wildlife.

The most extensive *deforestation* (clearing away of forests) is currently happening in the tropics. Scientists estimate that tropical rain forests currently cover less than 6% of the Earth's surface but provide homes to over 50% of the known *species* of plants and animals. Over 80% of all species of amphibians and reptiles live in the tropics. More than half of the area originally covered in rain forest has already been cut down.

It's hard to estimate how much tropical forest is destroyed each year, but conservative estimates suggest that about 50,400 square miles are cut each year. This figure is equivalent to the destruction of 29 city blocks of tropical forest per minute! Try to imagine an area of 29 city blocks in your city or town. Imagine this amount of tropical forest being cut down every minute!

At the current rate of deforestation, within 30 to 50 years most tropical forests will be gone. Haiti has already lost 99% of its original tropical forest. The Philippine Islands have lost 97%. Madagascar, home to 60% of the world's species of chameleons, has already lost 84% of its tropical forest.

Some tropical deforestation occurs because people need firewood, wood to build their homes, and land for farming. Sadly, however, much tropical deforestation is caused by human greed. We want more, and we want better. Tropical forests are cut down so that people can use exotic woods to make furniture. Huge areas of forest are converted to pasture for cattle. These cattle provide the meat for the hamburgers we buy in fast-food restaurants. Wherever precious minerals are found, the forest is destroyed so the minerals can be extracted from the earth. Roads are then carved into the forest so the minerals can be trucked out.

The first thing most settlers do when they move to the rain forest is cut down the forest and burn the undergrowth vegetation to clear their land, a process called slash-and-burn agriculture. Then they plant crops. Most tropical soils are not very fertile. After two or three years the nutrients in the soil are used up or rain has washed them away. Another problem is that when some tropical soils are exposed to direct sunlight, they harden and can't retain moisture. So, the farmers cut down more forest and clear more land for their crops. Just think of all the animals that lose their homes in the process!

Sometimes we destroy amphibian breeding sites just by modifying the environment, rather than by outright cutting down the forest. Most of us dislike mosquitoes, so we eliminate standing water where these pests lay their eggs. We replace drainage ditches with underground drainage systems. When we do this, mosquitoes aren't the only animals that lose their breeding sites: amphibians do also. The same thing happens when farmers and ranchers fill in their cattle-watering ponds and replace them with concrete or aluminum tanks, which are more efficient and convenient. Some treefrogs can scale the edges of the tanks and lay their eggs in the water, but other frogs and salamanders are out of luck.

INTRODUCTION OF EXOTIC SPECIES

When humans settle a new place we often take along our domesticated animals: pigs, cattle, sheep, and goats for food, and dogs and cats for companionship. Rats get introduced into new areas accidentally. These animals can have severe effects on native populations of amphibians and reptiles, especially on islands. In some cases the animals eat amphibians and reptiles or their eggs. In other cases they trample the habitat or compete with native amphibians and reptiles for food. Often these introduced animals don't have natural predators in their new environment, so they multiply quickly.

Galápagos tortoises have seriously declined over the past few centuries due to direct and indirect effects of people. Whereas once there were over 300,000 tortoises, there are only about 15,000 left now.

Tortoises on the Galápagos Islands in the Pacific have suffered greatly not only from the sailors who ate them but also from introduced animals. Rats, who came as stowaways on explorers' ships, greedily devour tortoise eggs and hatchlings. Goats, intentionally introduced onto the islands, compete with tortoises for food. Dogs and cats eat young tortoises.

Tuatara have disappeared from the two large islands and some of the smaller islands of New Zealand. Again, the causes are likely competition and predation from the sheep, goats, and rats introduced by early settlers.

In the 1870s, rats were such a problem in the sugarcane fields of Jamaica that mongooses were introduced from India to kill the rats. Mongooses don't eat only rats, however, and they don't always stay in cane fields. They also feast on birds and reptiles—in or outside cane fields. Mongooses wiped out or drastically reduced populations of several species of lizards and one species of snake in Jamaica.

Introduced amphibians and reptiles themselves can be a menace. A good example is the brown tree snake, unintentionally introduced onto the island of Guam, a territory of the United States, about halfway between Japan and New Guinea. The snake probably arrived hidden in cargo, about 50 years ago. Brown tree snakes have reproduced so successfully on the island that in some places there are now as many as 50 brown tree snakes in an area the size of a football field. Over time, the snake invaders have drastically reduced the populations of many species of birds and extinguished at least seven. Once it was hard to find birds, the snakes switched to lizards. By now they've greatly reduced or wiped out several species of lizards as well, especially the native geckos.

Bullfrogs were introduced west of the Rocky Mountains beginning in the 1800s for human food. Unfortunately, bullfrogs have voracious appetites, and in places where they were introduced many of the native species of frogs have disappeared. In many places of the world, bullfrogs are raised on "farms." Inevitably some escape. Once free, they devour the local amphibians.

Other *aquatic* invaders have caused the decline or disappearance of amphibians. Trout have been introduced into many rivers and lakes worldwide, both as a source of food and for recreation. Because trout love to eat tadpoles, stream- or lake-breeding frogs soon decline in areas where trout have been introduced. Tiny mosquitofish, introduced into many areas to control mosquitoes, don't eat only mosquito larvae. They also eat salamander larvae and tadpoles. Crayfish are another problem. Fishermen often buy live crayfish as bait and then dump the leftovers after fishing into the lake or stream. Although crayfish may not have occurred naturally in the lake or stream, these newcomers may thrive and breed—and eat amphibian eggs and larvae.

Another problem is that alien species such as bullfrogs, fish, and crayfish often carry parasites. Local amphibians can then be infected with these parasites, or catch diseases from these aliens as well.

ENVIRONMENTAL POLLUTION

Humans also affect amphibians and reptiles by polluting their habitat—air, water, and soil. Gasoline and oil wash off the roads and flow into the ground nearby. Pesticides and fertilizers seep into areas where amphibians and reptiles live. Chemicals from mining and logging operations and from industrial plants poison the land and the water. Some pollutants are carried long distances from one country to another in the air or in the water. Contaminants blow over from Africa to the Caribbean region, Central America, and northern South America. These different kinds of pollutants might directly kill amphibians and reptiles, or they might stunt their growth or affect reproduction.

One type of pollution that may harm amphibians comes from chemicals released in automobile exhaust and by factories that burn coal. Two such chemicals are nitrogen oxide and sulfur dioxide. The wind spreads these chemicals over wide areas. Mixed with water in the atmosphere, the chemicals turn to nitric acid and sulfuric acid. Rain then picks up these chemicals as it falls and becomes *acid rain*. Many amphibians can't tolerate acid conditions in their breeding ponds and lakes. Their eggs and larvae die, or they develop abnormally. Declines of some populations of tiger salamanders in the Rocky Mountains of Colorado and natterjack toads from Britain may be due to acid rain.

Chemical pollution may cause frogs to become deformed. During the mid-1990s, schoolchildren on fieldtrips found many deformed leopard frogs around farm ponds in Minnesota. These frogs had missing legs, twisted legs, stubby legs, extra legs, or double feet. Some frogs were missing an eye. People have found large numbers of deformed frogs elsewhere in the United States and in Canada within the past decade. What's causing the deformities? And at what stage are the frogs affected?

Perhaps it's something in the water that is affecting development of the eggs or tadpoles. The water might be contaminated by pesticides or poisonous heavy metals such as mercury and lead. Or perhaps the algae that the tadpoles eat contain toxic pollutants. Another possibility is that parasites may enter the developing legs of tadpoles and cause abnormalities. Maybe the deformities are caused by something on land—contaminated insects that the newly metamorphosed frogs eat, or toxic chemicals from the ground that are absorbed through the frogs' skin. At this point we don't have the answers and the investigations continue.

Some chemical pollutants interfere with the hormone systems of animals. Hormones are molecules produced by glands, released into the blood, and transported throughout the body. They serve as a chemical messenger system, and they influence various body functions. Medical researchers and biologists think that the hormone systems of many animals, including amphibians and reptiles, are being disrupted by chemical contamination in the environment.

One particularly nasty group of synthetic, toxic compounds are the polychlorinated biphenyls (PCBs for short). PCBs were once widely used in plastics, paints, and adhesives. In 1979, the U. S. government prohibited further production of PCBs and banned their use because medical research suggested that exposure to large amounts of PCBs was associated with birth defects, liver damage, and cancer in people. PCBs also cause reproductive failure in fishes, birds, and mammals. Unfortunately, PCBs stay in the environment a long time and are transported long distances through the air. Traces of PCBs are still found in air, soil, ocean, and animal tissues in the United States, even though they haven't been used for more than 20 years.

Some PCB compounds are so similar to estrogen (a hormone that affects female characteristics and behavior) that they act like estrogen when they get into an animal's body. One study of red-eared slider turtles showed that PCBs can change the sex of embryos that are developing into males. Instead of males, the embryos develop into females! If only females were produced, the population would soon go extinct.

Another type of pollution is solid waste. Think about the amount of garbage your family produces every week. Where does it go? Some of it might be recycled, but much gets buried in the ground, in landfills. Until 1992, the United States dumped millions of tons of waste, including chemicals, household trash, human waste from sewerage systems, plastics, and industrial waste, into the oceans each year. We thought it didn't cause any harm in the oceans because we assumed the oceans were large enough to absorb it. The marine animals have to live (or die) with it, though. Fortunately, since 1992 it has been illegal to dump wastes into the ocean. Some of the trash that's already there will last a long time, however. A tin can will last 50 years, and an aluminum soda can will last 200 years in the ocean.

Plastic was one common form of solid waste dumped into the oceans—an estimated 24,000 tons each year. Leatherback sea turtles eat mainly jellyfish, and a floating plastic bag resembles a jellyfish. In some areas, half the leatherbacks examined have plastic garbage in their intestines. The plastic probably interferes with the turtles' ability to digest food and to breathe. Some plastics are toxic and may be slowly poisoning the turtles. Unfortunately, plastics will litter the ocean for a long time because they break down slowly. Disposable diapers and plastic bottles will last about 450 years in the ocean.

10

WHO TURNED UP THE HEAT?

For 30 years climatologists (scientists who study the Earth's weather conditions) have warned that temperatures across the planet are getting warmer. We're living in times of "global warming." They predict that within the next 20 years, average temperatures will be warmer than at any other time during the past 1000 years. Warmer temperatures could cause change in deserts, wetlands, and forests: In some areas they might expand in size; in others, they might shrink. If ice melts in the Arctic and Antarctic, sea levels might rise and flood coastal habitats such as mangrove swamps.

Humans are to blame for much of this warming trend. We release huge amounts of heat-trapping gases, especially carbon dioxide, into the atmosphere when we burn oil, coal, and natural gas. Trees and other plants absorb carbon dioxide, so when we cut down forests, there are fewer plants to absorb it and the amount of this gas in the Earth's atmosphere increases. With more of this gas in the atmosphere, less heat is able to escape into space. This process is called the "greenhouse effect" because the Earth's atmosphere traps heat much like the glass or plastic walls and roof of a greenhouse.

Along with warmer temperatures, climatologists also predict that: (1) soils will become drier; (2) dry seasons will last longer; (3) the amount of rainfall will vary more from year to year; and (4) some areas will get more rain than normal, others will get less. Global warming and drier—or more variable—conditions will probably occur gradually over our lifetimes.

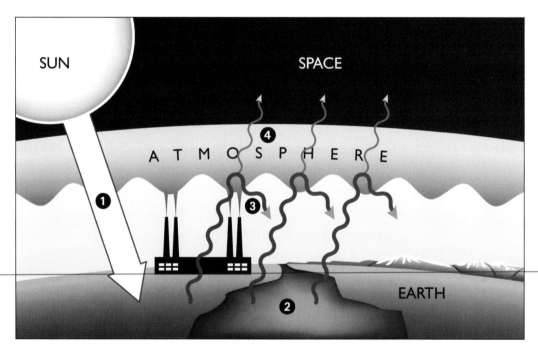

In the greenhouse effect, 1. Incoming heat energy from the sun warms Earth's surface. 2. Warmed surface radiates heat energy toward space. 3. Greenhouse gases trap and reradiate heat energy back toward Earth keeping the surface warm. 4. Limited amounts of heat escape from Earth's atmosphere.

How can amphibians and reptiles respond to warmer, and often drier, conditions? They can move into more suitable habitats. They can stay where they are and adapt to the changing conditions. Or they can die.

Few amphibians and reptiles can follow the first option. Some small salamanders and lizards don't roam more than 10 feet from the center of their *home range* (the area within which an animal moves about in its daily activities to find food and shelter) within their lifetimes. These animals almost certainly won't be able to move into a better habitat. Frogs that normally travel a mile or more in search of breeding ponds may be more able to move, but only if they don't encounter barriers, such as dry fields. In general, snakes and turtles move around more than lizards and amphibians do. Some big turtles and snakes have home ranges larger than 50 acres (the area of about 40 football fields). In theory, animals that travel far in search of food could migrate in search of a better habitat. But we're destroying habitat, so in reality, they too will encounter barriers such as roads and cities that may prevent them from reaching cooler or wetter places.

If climate changes happen gradually, over many lifetimes of amphibians and reptiles, some *populations* may be able to adapt. Not all amphibians and reptiles are equally *adaptable*, however. Adaptability is the ability to adjust to changes. Garter snakes are adaptable. They can live in many different habitats, including city parks and around people's homes, because they tolerate a wide range of temperatures and eat a wide variety of prey. If the average temperature this year is half a degree warmer than last year, it's no big deal for them. If fewer frogs are out and about because the climate is drier, garter snakes will eat grasshoppers and other insects instead.

Some amphibians and reptiles are *specialized,* though. That is, they can survive only within a narrow set of environmental conditions. They may tolerate only a certain range of temperature and humidity, or perhaps they eat only ants. Specialized *species* have a hard time coping with environmental change, such as warmer, drier conditions. The golden toads of Costa Rica were probably very specialized. They lived only in one small area of cloud forest, under the tree roots where normally plenty of water existed. When an unusual drought came, the toads may have been unable to tolerate the dry soil, and they had nowhere else to go.

There isn't much to say about the third option: death. Animals that can't or don't move elsewhere may die if they can't adapt to climatic changes.

Warmer, drier conditions might affect individual amphibians and reptiles in many ways. Here are some possibilities and some questions to ponder:

- There might be less food for species that eat small insects. Many small insects can't survive dry conditions, so they'll die. Other insects might hide out in cooler, wetter places where they're hard to find. What will amphibians and reptiles find to eat?

- Activity patterns might change. Some species might be active more hours each day, and more days each year. Other species might be less active because they can't tolerate the warmer temperatures. How will interactions among species change?

- Warmer, drier conditions might cause physical stress to amphibians and reptiles and depress their immune systems. Will they become more vulnerable to diseases?

- With less rain, ponds would hold water for less time. So when there is water, all the frogs might come to lay eggs at once. The result would be hundreds of thousands of tadpoles in a pond. Will there be enough food for them to develop into froglets?

- Amphibians that lay their eggs on land might have trouble finding moist sites. Once they find them, will the sites dry up before the eggs hatch? Reptile eggs might die also if the air is too dry.

- Warmer temperatures might change the numbers of males versus females that are born. In many reptiles, the incubation temperature of the eggs determines whether the hatchlings will be male or female. In some species, warm temperatures cause embryos to become female and cool temperatures cause embryos to become male. In other species, the pattern is reversed: Embryos incubated at warm temperatures become male and those at cool temperatures become female. How would birth of all males or all females affect the future of these species?

Another change that may affect amphibians, and perhaps also reptiles, is an increase in the amount of UV (ultraviolet) radiation from the sun that's reaching Earth's surface. Ultraviolet rays are both good and bad for animals. They stimulate bone growth, but they also cause sunburn and encourage development of skin cancer. You smear sunscreen on yourself to shield your skin from the UV rays. Ultraviolet radiation can slowly cause blindness. You wear sunglasses to block out the UV rays from your eyes. Exposure to high levels of UV rays can also damage amphibians' eyes, and they can't put on sunglasses. Many amphibians lay their eggs in shallow water where the sun heats up the water and allows the eggs to develop quickly. The bad part of being exposed to direct sunlight is that high doses of UV radiation can cause amphibian embryos to develop abnormally and even die. The amphibians that appear to be suffering the most from increased UV radiation live at high elevations in the mountains where the rays are much stronger than at lower elevations.

Sometimes the amount of UV radiation striking frog or salamander eggs isn't enough by itself to cause damage. Increased UV radiation, however, can make the eggs more vulnerable to fungus infection. Ultimately, the embryos die from the fungus. There might also be an interaction between UV radiation and acid rain. Either factor alone might not kill amphibian eggs, but the combination could be lethal.

Ultraviolet radiation is a bigger problem now than it was 30 years ago. Why? The *ozone* (a form of oxygen) layer in the upper atmosphere of Earth is becoming thinner each year. The ozone layer normally blocks out most UV radiation, serving as our global sunscreen. With a thinner ozone layer, more UV radiation comes through and strikes Earth's surface.

Chemicals called chlorofluorocarbons, CFCs for short, are responsible for much of the thinning. CFCs are compounds of chlorine, fluorine, and carbon. These compounds don't smell and you can't see them. They're used as cooling substances in refrigerators and air conditioners; in cleaning agents and plastic foams; and as propellants in aerosol spray cans. Every time someone sprays deodorant or insect repellent from an aerosol can containing these chemicals, CFCs are released into the air. About 25 years ago scientists discovered that CFCs float up into the ozone layer. There, UV rays strike these chemicals. The CFCs break apart and release chlorine. The atoms of chlorine react with ozone and change the ozone to ordinary oxygen, which doesn't have the UV-screening abilities of ozone.

Since the late 1970s, the United States, Canada, and many other countries have banned the use of CFCs in aerosol spray cans. Unfortunately, however, CFCs are still used in aerosol cans manufactured in other countries and are still used for other purposes as well. More than 100 nations are working together to reduce the amount of CFCs released into the air. Even if CFCs were completely banned today, though, we'd still have a problem: CFCs are hard to break down, and they float around in the air for a long time. Some scientists estimate that about 95% of the CFCs released since 1955 are still making their way up to destroy the ozone layer. Thus, even if all CFCs were banned today, damage to our sunscreen layer may continue throughout the twenty-first century.

GOOD OR BAD? LOVE OR HATE?

The actions of people may be causing some amphibians and reptiles to decline and others to disappear. People can also be the solution to the problem, though. How do we start? We begin by improving the way people feel about amphibians and reptiles.

Conservation organizations spend millions of dollars each year to protect furry pandas, huge whales and elephants, and human-like gorillas and chimpanzees. This is necessary, and it's good. But they often ignore amphibians and reptiles. In fact, out of each dollar spent on conservation of wildlife, less than a nickel is spent on amphibians and reptiles. Why?

Attitudes toward amphibians and reptiles are mixed. Many people think these animals aren't worth worrying about. Others think amphibians and reptiles are ugly and boring, or they're afraid of them. The words "amphibians" and "reptiles" are even associated with bad people. One definition of reptile in my dictionary is "a groveling, sneaky, very mean person." And one definition of toad is "a despicable person."

Toads and snakes have other bad word associations. Have you heard the expression, "ugly as a toad?" Or "mean as a snake?" To "toady" up to someone, or to "toadeat," means to flatter a person to get into their good graces. A "snake in the grass" is someone who seems harmless but is actually evil or dangerous. The expression "lower than a snake's belly" refers to something really mean or nasty.

Fortunately, not everyone shares these negative views. Many people besides *herpetologists* think that amphibians and reptiles are fascinating. Consider the following examples of people's attitudes that reflect good or bad, love or hate.

All over the world, people worship frogs as symbols of fertility, no doubt because many *species* lay thousands of eggs. They're also honored for their resurrection abilities—frogs appear seemingly out of nowhere after a hard rain. (They're ready to breed!) Many people believe that frogs have supernatural powers, probably because of their "magical" *metamorphosis* from the tadpole stage into a four-legged frog. For the same reason, frogs are often symbols of creation. Many people wear amulets (charms) of frogs for good luck. On the negative side, many people believe that toads cause warts, so they're afraid to touch "the ugly creatures!" Toads often symbolize ugliness in literature and folktales.

On the South Pacific island of New Caledonia, people don't kill lizards because they believe lizards might carry their own ancestors' souls. In contrast, Iranians often kill lizards because they believe lizards carry the devil's soul. Some people from Thailand hate monitor lizards because they believe that monitors dig up graves and eat human flesh.

On Mindanao in the Philippine Islands, locals hesitate to live in thatched huts where there are no geckos. They figure that if geckos aren't there, something must be wrong with the place. In Thailand, people don't want geckos in their homes because they believe geckos bring bad luck. Just think how differently people in Mindanao versus Thailand would feel if you suddenly appeared and asked that the local geckos be protected. People on Mindanao would agree, and they probably would be glad to help. Thai people would be horrified and less likely to cooperate.

Because of their strong shells, turtles seem well designed to carry burdens on their backs. Perhaps this explains the stories from parts of India, China, Japan, and North and South America that huge turtles support the mountains and even entire continents. People from these cultures respect turtles. Some North Americans believe that if you keep a turtle in your garden, it'll bring you good luck. In contrast, tribes in some parts of the Amazon Basin believe turtles to be evil so they kill them.

In parts of Madagascar, people worship crocodiles because they believe these reptiles possess the spirits of former chiefs. In Borneo, people generally protect crocodiles because they believe crocodiles can drive away evil spirits. Ancient Egyptians believed that crocodiles were sacred, and in fact they built the holy city of Crocodilopolis to honor them. Egyptians cared for crocodiles at their temples and they even mummified and buried them after their pets died. Not everyone respects crocodilians, though. In some parts of the world people believe that the only good thing about a crocodilian is its skin or its flesh. Many people believe that all alligators and crocodiles are man-eaters, so they kill every one possible to make the environment safe.

Snakes symbolize love and health in some cultures, even being considered the most honored of all mythical supernatural beings. Snakes also symbolize rejuvenation and immortality because they throw off their old skin and have a fresh one waiting underneath. Most native tribes in North America honored and protected rattlesnakes. People in parts of Africa protect pythons, worshipping them as gods and as ancestral spirits.

Snakes cause negative reactions too. This attitude goes back at least to the Book of Genesis in the Old Testament of the Bible. The serpent (snake) encourages Eve to eat the fruit that God has forbidden her. She gives some to Adam, and he also eats it. As a result, God expels Adam and Eve, the first two humans he created, from

A snake sheds its outer layer of skin because it wears out. An active snake may shed 6 or more times during the year, whereas a less active snake may shed only twice.

the Garden of Eden. They become mortal, meaning they will eventually die. As for the serpent, God curses it, saying:

> Because you have done this,
>   cursed are you above all cattle,
>   and above all wild animals;
> upon your belly you shall go,
>   and dust you shall eat
>   all the days of your life.

Some people point to this passage of the Bible as their excuse for thinking that snakes are evil.

Polls taken today indicate that North Americans fear snakes even more than they fear spiders, mice, or speaking in public. Fear of snakes often leads people to kill every one that they see.

* * *

Why is it important to know how people feel about amphibians and reptiles? Because once we understand, we can work to change negative attitudes. Once people appreciate amphibians and reptiles they'll be more willing to protect them.

Perhaps the greatest problem is that many people don't think of amphibians and reptiles at all. Like the trees, the air, the oceans and rivers, and like other animals, they are "just there." We go about our lives thinking only of what we need *now*, and we take amphibians and reptiles for granted. But this is a luxury we can't afford any longer.

WE CAN LIVE TOGETHER, CAN'T WE?

The single most important way we can help amphibians and reptiles is by protecting the environment. How can we do this when there are so many human demands on the land? By compromising. And by suggesting alternatives. Realistically, it's difficult to change the behavior of people associated with huge logging and mining operations. But we can influence the way individuals use their land.

Conservationists can't go charging into Latin America, or anywhere else, and demand that people stop their slash-and-burn agriculture in order to save the rain forest. Conservationists must consider the needs of the local people. Perhaps slash-and-burn agriculture is the only way the colonists know how to support their families. If they learn alternative ways of earning a living, perhaps they could stop destroying the rain forest. Local people must see habitat protection as a benefit to them if it is going to work.

Conservationists are currently working with people in local communities, experimenting with alternative ways of earning a living in the rain forest without cutting down trees. Nuts are being harvested and carved into buttons. Fruits and nuts are being gathered for food. Oils and fibers are being extracted from trees. Once trees are viewed as more valuable if left unharmed, the forest will remain intact.

PRESERVATION OF LAND

When possible, of course, it's ideal to set aside huge areas of land. For example, governments and *conservation* organizations can buy land for national parks and reserves. It's not enough to set the land aside, however. The park or reserve, as well as the plants and animals within the boundaries, must be protected from poachers, loggers, and miners. It's getting harder and harder to buy up big tracts of forest, however, because of increasing human demands on the land.

National Wildlife Refuges have been established in various places in the United States. These refuges are the only network of federal lands and water that are managed mainly for the protection of animals. Most of the refuges were established to protect birds and mammals, but at least 9 were set up mainly with amphibians and reptiles in mind. For example:

- Coachella Valley National Wildlife Refuge, California: protection of Coachella Valley fringe-toed lizard

- Ellicott Slough National Wildlife Refuge, California: protection of Santa Cruz long-toed salamander

- Archie Carr National Wildlife Refuge, Florida: protection of green sea turtle and loggerhead sea turtle

- Crocodile Lake National Wildlife Refuge, Florida: protection of American crocodile

- Massasoit National Wildlife Refuge, Massachusetts: protection of Plymouth red-bellied turtle

- Mortenson Lake National Wildlife Refuge, Wyoming: protection of Wyoming toad

One of the reasons tropical forests are cut down is that developing countries sell off their forests for lumber to get quick cash so they can pay off their debts. Developing countries borrow money from international banks to fund projects such as building dams and roads. Worldwide, developing countries owe these banks a total of about 1.3 trillion dollars. When it comes time to repay their loans, the easiest way is often to exploit their natural resources, such as forests. Many of these countries have severe economic problems and they'll never be able to pay back these loans.

Conservationists came up with the "debt-for-nature swap" program in the mid-1980s as a partial solution to this predicament. The program works as follows. A conservation organization works with a developing country to design a conservation project. For example, the project might be to protect a tract of rain forest where endangered monkeys live. The conservation organization then buys part of the debt of that developing country at a greatly discounted price from the banks. The banks are willing to do this because they know they'll never see the debt repaid by the developing country anyway. The developing country doesn't have to pay back this part of the debt. In return, the country supports the preservation of the land for the monkeys. Of course, many amphibians, reptiles, and other animals live in that rain forest, so they'll be protected also.

The first of these debt-for-nature swaps began in Bolivia, in 1987. In return for not having to pay back $650,000 of the money it owed, Bolivia created the Beni Biosphere Reserve. These 3.7 million acres of rain forest provide protection for parrots, macaws, jaguars, monkeys, anacondas, side-necked turtles, treefrogs, caecilians, and all the other animals and plants in the area. The organization Conservation International bought the Bolivian debt for a mere $100,000. Since then, debt-for-nature swaps have been carried out in several other countries, including Ecuador, Costa Rica, Mexico, the Philippine Islands, and Madagascar.

One way of protecting private land in the United States is through *conservation easements*—agreements on how private land will be used. The agreement is made between the government or a conservation organization and the landowner. If the land is especially valuable for plants and animals, the landowner receives money or perhaps a tax benefit in return for not developing the land. Here's how this might work:

A rancher owns 1000 acres of cattle pasture. His other 200 acres are swampland, which he's considering filling in with sand and converting into a shopping mall. The town nearby votes for the mall, and the rancher wouldn't mind having all the extra money. But he feels guilty because he promised his granddad that he would keep the land undeveloped. The local conservation organization argues against development because rare salamanders live in the swamp. The rancher and members of the conservation group strike a deal: They set up a conservation easement. In return for not developing the land, the rancher receives a lump sum of money.

The protected land benefits not only the rare salamanders but also all the other plants and animals that live there. Everyone is happy— except the townspeople who didn't get their mall.

SHARING THE EARTH

Some amphibians and reptiles, such as Komodo dragons, require huge areas of land away from people. To protect Komodo dragons, we need to set aside land for them. Other animals, though, have life styles more compatible with the presence of people. Instead of setting aside land for them, we need to change how we use the environment so we can coexist better. Following are some examples of how we can do this.

WE CAN HELP ANIMALS TO CROSS ROADS SAFELY. Some toads live in the forest most of the year. After heavy rains in the spring, they migrate to ponds to lay their eggs. Afterwards, the toads return to the forest where they stay until the next breeding season. What happens if a road is built between the forest and the pond? To get to the pond, the toads will have to cross the road. Many will never make it to the other side. They'll be squashed flat by cars and trucks.

Australian scientists estimate that nearly 5.5 million amphibians and reptiles are killed on paved roads each year in their country! Imagine how many are squashed on roads every year throughout the world. Just in the United States, we have over 3.8 million miles of public roads. About 200 million vehicles travel these roads.

Concerned citizens have developed ways of reducing the numbers of animals killed on roads. In some areas in Europe and North

America, road signs warn motorists about migrations of toads and salamanders. Motorists are asked not to use these roads during the toad and salamander breeding seasons. If the roads must be used, motorists are asked to drive slowly and avoid the animals.

In some places engineers build tunnels under roads to connect important habitats for amphibians and reptiles. They construct barriers along both sides of the road so that animals can't walk, hop, crawl, or slither onto the pavement. The animals turn right or left and follow along the barrier until they find an opening—the tunnel. Once through the tunnel, they've safely crossed the road and can continue on their way. These tunnels have prevented the slaughter of thousands of frogs, toads, salamanders, snakes, and turtles.

Where there are no tunnels, human volunteers do the job. Adults and kids collect toads in buckets and carry them safely across roads. They call themselves "toad patrols." In the United Kingdom, toad patrols at more than 400 sites save an estimated 500,000 toads each year. Some communities in Canada and the United States also have toad patrols. Get your friends together and form a toad patrol. It's fun!

WE CAN DIG PONDS FOR AMPHIBIANS. People try to simplify their lives, but in the process sometimes other animals get hurt. For example, in one area of the Netherlands much of the land is used for cattle pastures. In the early 1900s, the area had over 1000 cattle-watering ponds. Salamanders, frogs, and toads used these ponds for breeding. During the past 30 years, ranchers have replaced many of these ponds with concrete drinking basins and automatic self-drink devices for the cows. With fewer breeding ponds, 2 of the 12 *species* of amphibians once present have disappeared and another 5 are declining. Fortunately, concerned people have come to the rescue. They're digging new ponds for the amphibians.

Midwife toads in Spain have also declined because ranchers have replaced cattle-watering ponds with modern watering devices. Midwife toads get their name because the males carry the eggs entwined around their waists and thighs until the eggs are just about ready to hatch. At that point the dads hop into water and the hatchlings burst forth from their egg capsules. If there's no water available for Dad to hop into, the eggs dry up and die before they can hatch. It would indeed be sad to lose these unique frogs. Help is on the way, though. Men, women, and children are digging ponds for the toads.

Do you know an area that could use a frog pond? If so, begin by talking with your teacher. Perhaps he or she can organize a class project.

WE CAN TURN OUT THE LIGHTS FOR BABY TURTLES. Female sea turtles crawl out of the ocean and lay their eggs in holes they dig on the beach. The eggs incubate in the warm sand, and eventually the baby sea turtles hatch. The hatchlings usually dig their way out at night. After emerging, they make a beeline for the ocean. How do they know which way the water is? Hatchling turtles instinctively head for the brightest horizon. Normally the brightest light comes from moonlight or starlight reflected off the surface of the ocean. When people build homes close to the ocean, the lights shining from these buildings confuse the baby turtles. Instead of heading for the ocean, the turtles head inland, toward the lights from the buildings. Many dry up in the sun the next day or are run over by cars and trucks.

Many communities along the beaches of the southeastern United States now have rules about turning lights off during the sea turtle nesting season. For example, along turtle nesting beaches in Florida, lights are generally allowed only until 11:00 at night. After 11:00 p.m., without artificial lights to confuse them, the baby turtles orient correctly and make it to the ocean. The ones that emerge before 11:00 p.m. are the unlucky ones.

WE CAN HELP SEA TURTLES ESCAPE FROM SHRIMP NETS. In the United States, a major cause of death for sea turtles is from

The TED in this shrimp net is being tested to make sure it works properly. One diver is videotaping the test (the line you see is a camera line attached to a boat). The other diver is timing the test. If the turtle doesn't escape within 5 minutes, the TED fails and the divers release the turtle. *Photo by Ian K. Workman. Courtesy of National Marine Fisheries Service/NOAA*

drowning in the nets that fishermen use to catch shrimp. In fact, more sea turtles die in these nets than from all other human-caused sources of death combined. Some years more than 60,000 die in shrimp nets. Once entangled in the nets, the turtles can't swim to the surface for air. They often drown in less than an hour.

A clever contraption, called a turtle excluder device (TED), was designed in the early 1980s as a solution. A TED is a small net or metal cage-like device that's sewn into the throat of a shrimp net. It allows shrimp to be caught in the net, but allows turtles to escape. The turtle's body flips through a trapdoor and back into the open ocean. The best TEDs allow about 97% of the turtles caught to escape. Since the mid-1990s, shrimpers in the United States are now required by the federal government to use TEDs, and conservation organizations even offer to pay for them. This is just one more way that we can share the Earth with amphibians and reptiles.

13

RESEARCH AND EDUCATION

After habitat protection and sharing the environment, the two most important ways we can protect amphibians and reptiles are by learning more about them and by educating people about the importance and value of these animals.

RESEARCH

Does anyone reading this book want to be a biologist? A *conservation* biologist? A conservation biologist who works with amphibians and reptiles? For anyone who answered "yes" to these questions, there's a lot of work for you.

We need more research to understand how we can best protect amphibians and reptiles. This includes what they eat and who their predators are, information about their social behavior, reproductive patterns, habitat preferences, and the sizes of their *populations*.

In order to protect a habitat for a certain *species,* we need to know what habitat that species uses. Does it spend all of its life in the forest? Or does it migrate between swampland and forest? Research will answer these questions.

Semi-*aquatic* turtles live in wetlands. They spend much of their time in the water, but they wander to higher ground to lay their eggs on land. Federal laws protect wetlands and a little dry land around them by prohibiting development within the area. But scientists have found that sometimes not enough land is protected as a buffer zone.

Research on turtles in a wetland in South Carolina showed that all of the turtles' nesting sites and all of their hibernation burrows were on dry land *outside* the protected area. Obviously, the laws were not adequate for protecting these turtles. What if a developer had built an apartment complex near the wetland—the perfect place for residents to watch turtles basking on logs? Where would the turtles lay their eggs? And where would they hibernate in the winter? Now that research has shown that the turtles need more land for their nesting and hibernation activities, conservation biologists can argue that the federal regulations need to be changed.

We also need research to be sure we're protecting the right stages of animals. To protect sea turtles, should we focus on the eggs, the baby turtles, or the adults? To determine which age group needs the most protection, we need information on the chance of dying and the major causes of death at each stage. Sea turtles live a long time. Each female lays hundreds of eggs, but most of the eggs and baby turtles die because there are so many predators that eat them. In some species, fewer than 1% of the eggs ever become adult turtles. Since so many eggs and baby turtles will die no matter what, conservation efforts should focus mainly on subadults and adults.

We learned this lesson the hard way with Kemp's ridley, the world's most *endangered* sea turtle. Biologists spent over 14 years (1978–1992) and more than $4 million protecting eggs on the nesting beach in Mexico, transporting the eggs to the United States, and then raising the young in a laboratory safe from predators. Over time, the biologists released more than 20,000 babies (9–12 months old) into the coastal waters of Texas and Florida. But after all those years of protection, there aren't many more Kemp's ridleys now than there were when the project began. Why? Because so many adult turtles drown in shrimp nets. The best way to protect Kemp's ridleys is to require shrimp fishermen to use turtle excluder devices. U. S. fishermen are now required to do so, and, as of 1993, Mexico requires its shrimp fishermen in the Gulf of Mexico and Caribbean waters to use TEDs. Scientists are optimistic that the species may be in the early phase of recovery.

For many species of amphibians and reptiles we don't know how much space individuals need to carry out their daily activities, such as foraging for food. If we want to set aside land to protect anacondas, we'll need a much larger area than if we wish to set aside land for an endangered salamander. But how much more land?

How many individual anacondas must there be in the preserve for them to be able to find each other and breed successfully? How many individual salamanders do we need in our smaller preserve for them to be able to breed successfully? These are questions that can be answered only with more research.

Scientists worldwide are carrying out research to unravel what's going on with the worldwide declines and disappearances of amphibians. They're establishing long-term monitoring programs to document which species are declining, and they're studying the possible causes of the disappearances. Some of these studies include experiments with UV radiation, acid water, fungus, and other diseases.

EDUCATION

"Please Brake for Snakes" reads the diamond-shaped sign posted in Killbear Provincial Park in Ontario, Canada. The sign reaches out to park visitors as part of a project to promote conservation of the eastern massasauga rattlesnake. These shy and non-aggressive snakes are declining in Ontario and the United States because people are destroying their habitat and killing the snakes. In Killbear Provincial Park, as many rattlesnakes are killed by cars as are eaten by natural predators. Thus the sign.

Since 1992 Chris Parent has studied these snakes and has been changing people's attitudes toward Ontario's only *venomous* snake. Chris and park personnel offer snake talks for campers of the park. People's attitudes quickly change from fear to respect. People come into the talk thinking that rattlesnakes lie in wait for the chance to strike people. They leave the talk realizing that instead of these snakes threatening us, we are threatening them. The conservation message is that the 250,000 annual human *visitors* to the park can safely coexist with the 200 to 300 rattlesnakes that *live* there.

The rattlesnake education project has been extremely successful. Many residents of the area who once killed every rattlesnake they saw, now carefully sweep the snakes into overturned garbage cans—and call the park staff so that data can be collected on the locations and activities of the snakes. Most amazing is the cooperation from visitors to the park. When campers report a rattlesnake, the park staff catch it and record data. Afterwards, the staff ask the campers for permission to relocate the snake within 500 yards (sometimes less than 100 yards) of its capture site. The campers have veto power, but they nearly always agree to the release. Thanks to what they've learned about rattlesnakes, the campers know that the snake makes that area its home and that's where it should be. That's an effective education program!

• • •

Recently, many countries have realized that tourists will pay lots of money to see wildlife under natural conditions. Tourists pay entrance fees to get into a reserve. They also spend money on hiring local guides, buying food and souvenirs, and staying in local hotels. All of this enriches the local economy. So, instead of allowing timber companies to cut down their forests, governments and local communities are setting aside protected land and encouraging *ecotourism*—tourism based on natural history.

Africa has some of the world's most popular nature reserves, where you can see lions, giraffes, and zebras. But ecotourism focusing on amphibians and reptiles is also popular. You can go to Costa Rica or Florida and watch sea turtles come ashore to lay their eggs. You can travel to the exotic island of Komodo in Indonesia and spy on the daily activities of Komodo dragons. In fact, this is becoming more common. In 1992, about 300 foreign tourists visited Komodo National Park. Two years later the figure jumped to over 30,000. Another popular activity for ecotourists is photographing marine

Ecotourists can get close to marine iguanas on the Galápagos Islands because the lizards are unafraid of people. They've lived for so long without predators that they don't view people as a threat.

iguanas and giant tortoises on the Galápagos Islands off the coast of Ecuador.

Ecotourism provides a great opportunity to educate the public both about the animals they're watching and the need for conservation of these animals and their habitats. Carefully controlled ecotourism can protect habitat and wildlife and at the same time improve people's attitudes about nature. Ecotourism also provides a unique opportunity for local people to participate in the teaching as well as the learning part of the education process. Local people can help construct displays, distribute pamphlets and newsletters, produce radio and television programs, and work as guides and park guards in their reserve.

Another way of educating the public is to include nonscientists in research projects, such as monitoring the status of endangered or declining amphibians and reptiles. In one Canadian project, pairs of people are responsible for monitoring the number of frogs at breeding sites. Each pair surveys their pond one rainy night per month. It's great fun for the participants, and many more ponds are surveyed than if one investigator were to do it alone. Once nonscientists become involved, they become more interested in the animals. They spread the word and educate others.

Nonscientists are needed as volunteers throughout the world to help with conservation projects. One exciting opportunity involves the Utila iguana, a large lizard found only on the island of Utila, off the coast of Honduras in Central America. This impressive iguana is threatened with extinction, largely because local people hunt the pregnant females and eat their eggs. Scientists have developed an extensive public education program, which includes a field station, to teach the locals about their unique iguana and the importance of not hunting them. Volunteers help in many phases of the project, including the field research and caring for the captive iguanas at the field station.

You don't need to visit foreign countries to learn about amphibians and reptiles and their need for conservation. And you don't need to help a scientist with his or her study. You can watch amphibians and reptiles in your own backyard or nearby woods. When you have questions, go to the library or talk with your parents or your teacher. Share what you learn with others. The more educated you become, the more you can convince others of the importance in conserving these animals.

14

WHAT ELSE CAN BE DONE?

Although habitat protection, research, and education are critical, there are additional ways of protecting amphibians and reptiles. Laws can be effective if they're rigidly enforced. We can move animals into areas where *populations* of a particular *species* have disappeared. Instead of collecting amphibians and reptiles from the wild and killing them for skins or food or selling them for pets, we can raise animals in captivity for the same purposes. We can use fewer animals for dissections. We can regulate legal hunting of amphibians and reptiles so that populations don't decline or go extinct.

LAWS THAT PROTECT AMPHIBIANS AND REPTILES

Each country is different in how much it protects amphibians and reptiles. Some countries protect no species at all. At the other extreme is Belgium. There, all amphibians and reptiles except for two common species of frogs have been protected for over 25 years.

Of course, just having laws isn't enough. The laws must be enforced. There are lots of examples where laws aren't much good. Here's one: All amphibians are protected by law in Romania. If you want to collect a frog for any reason, you need a permit. Unfortunately for the frogs, it's fairly easy to get a permit and commercial frog hunters have discovered just how easy it is. In 1998, about 20 tons of water frogs were exported from Romania, their legs destined for gourmet meals.

In 1973, the United States passed the Endangered Species Act, a law that protects both U. S. and foreign wildlife classified as either *endangered* or *threatened*. Endangered species are those that are in danger of extinction throughout all or most of their range. Threatened species are those that are likely to become endangered within the near future. Once a species is listed as either endangered or threatened, scientists develop a recovery plan. This plan might involve buying and preserving critical habitat, breeding the species in captivity, relocating animals to a different area, and/or doing additional research.

As of December 2001, 34 species of amphibians and 118 reptiles are protected under the U. S. Endangered Species Act. Of these, 104 are considered endangered and 48 are considered threatened. If a person is caught killing or taking an endangered or threatened species from the wild, he or she can be fined or thrown into jail—unless that person has a permit for scientific study. The Endangered Species Act also protects critical habitat needed by endangered and threatened species, so it's against the law to destroy the habitat used by any of these protected species.

Also in 1973, an international endangered species treaty was drafted by 81 nations—the Convention on International Trade in Endangered Species of Wild Fauna and Flora (CITES). The CITES treaty protects wildlife and plants throughout the world by making it illegal to sell endangered species, live or dead, to another country. Because it is now illegal to import endangered species, poachers have no legal market for their illegally captured parrots, monkeys, or boas. The CITES treaty also protects species that biologists think might become endangered. These species can be collected and sold only if the proper permits are obtained. As of November 2001, 155 countries have signed the CITES treaty. The treaty protects about 600 species of reptiles and amphibians in addition to many thousands of other animals and plants. Unfortunately, CITES deals only with buying and selling of wildlife across international borders. It does not apply to trade within countries.

These laws sound good, but once again they're only as good as their enforcement. And they are difficult to enforce. About 30% of the world's trade in wildlife is estimated to be in violation of CITES and national laws.

REESTABLISH POPULATIONS IN THE WILD

Sometimes when a population disappears, we can move animals from elsewhere and reestablish the population.

Imagine the following scene in southern California. The ground is dry and hard. The ponds are mere basins of cracked mud. Two years ago was a record dry summer. The next summer was almost as dry. An endangered treefrog has disappeared from the area. The third summer, rains return in full force. The ponds fill with water. But no treefrogs come to breed. Is this population gone forever? Not necessarily.

Frogs might migrate in from nearby areas and colonize these ponds on their own. If not, biologists can take charge and do the job by collecting frogs from nearby areas and releasing them at the site. This makes sense if the reason for the disappearance is a natural event, such as unusual weather. But would it make sense to relocate animals to an area that was formerly a forest but is now a subdivision packed with homes? No. Can you think of other instances where it wouldn't make sense to try and reestablish populations?

Gopher tortoises live in dry, sandy areas in the coastal plains of the United States between South Carolina and Louisiana. They dig and live in burrows about 13 feet long. Because they need dry areas for their burrows, the tortoises prefer the areas that humans also prefer for building their homes, office buildings, and shopping malls. Humans are more powerful, so we take the land and displace the tortoises. As a result, populations of gopher tortoises are dwindling, even though these tortoises are protected in much of their range as a threatened species by the Endangered Species Act.

What's a developer to do if gopher tortoises live on land he or she plans to convert to condominiums? Some states require the developer to move the tortoises to another appropriate habitat. Biologists choose substitute areas based on knowledge of the tortoises' feeding and habitat requirements, and then they relocate the tortoises.

Moving wild animals from one place to another isn't always the perfect solution, however. One problem is that sometimes the animals don't stay where we put them. They wander off until they find what *they* consider to be prime real estate. Another problem, especially if the animals have spent time in captivity, is that the former captives can spread disease to wild animals.

One way of reestablishing populations, called *head-starting*, involves hatching eggs in captivity. The hatchlings are raised to a size large enough so that when they're released into the wild they'll be less likely to be eaten by predators. Scientists are currently using head-starting programs to reestablish populations of some amphibians, lizards, turtles and tortoises, crocodilians, and tuatara.

One success story is work being done at the Charles Darwin Research Station in the Galápagos Islands. There, workers raise

Baby Galápagos tortoises are raised from eggs in incubators. The babies are housed in outdoor pens until they are large enough that most predators can't eat them. At that point, usually between the ages of 4 and 5 years, they are released into the wild.

tortoises and land iguanas from eggs. Once the young reptiles grow to a reasonable size, the workers release them onto islands where predators are controlled. So far, the efforts seem to be working: Populations of tortoises and land iguanas appear to be increasing on these islands.

Another success story is a head-starting project with Utila iguanas, on Utila Island in Central America. In addition to the education program to teach locals not to hunt the pregnant females, biologists are breeding the lizards. Workers catch pregnant females from the nesting beaches and put them in large cages with sand. After the females lay their eggs, the workers set the lizards free. Safe from predators, most of the artificially incubated eggs hatch. The workers release half of the hatchlings in the mangrove swamps immediately. They raise the other half at the breeding station for a year, and then release them when they're large enough to be less vulnerable to predators, including birds, snakes, dogs, and cats.

CAPTIVE RAISING OF ANIMALS FOR SKINS, FOOD, AND PETS

Instead of killing or taking wild animals for skins, food, or pets, we can raise the animals in captivity. Then, once they're large enough the animals can be sold and a profit can be made.

There are two types of such businesses: farms and ranches. In a *farming operation,* people initially collect adult animals from the wild. They breed the adults on the farm and raise the eggs. The owners set aside some of the young for future breeding stock, and they kill and sell the rest. Unfortunately, because the farmers don't need any more animals from the wild, they have no incentive to protect wild populations or their natural habitat.

In a *ranching operation*, the workers take eggs or hatchlings from the wild and raise them in captivity to be sold later. Each year or so they collect more eggs or hatchlings from the wild. Because ranching depends on a continuing supply of wild animals, there is strong incentive to protect both the habitat and wild populations.

There are some success stories. Farms and ranches in Africa are producing high quality skins of Nile crocodiles. Eventually there should be enough skins from captive animals so that wild crocodiles will no longer be hunted.

Costa Ricans farm green iguanas and release the captive-raised juveniles into areas where green iguanas have been hunted out. Two or three years later, people can then hunt these iguanas for food. The project provides two benefits: *conservation* of declining populations of iguanas, and incentive to protect the tropical forest. If people want the young iguanas to grow large enough so they can hunt them, they've got to provide food—leaves from the treetops.

Many amphibians and reptiles that are popular as pets are now being farmed successfully: poison-dart frogs, horned frogs, leopard geckos, green iguanas, chameleons, bearded dragon lizards, pythons, and boas, to name but a few. Even Komodo dragons are successfully farmed and sold to zoos.

Not all animals can be raised in captivity successfully, though. Frog farming was once thought to be a way of satisfying the world's craving for frog legs. Bullfrog farms became popular in the United States, Japan, Brazil, Ecuador, Argentina, and other countries. Bullfrogs grow very slowly, however, and it's hard to provide enough live food for the bullfrogs' voracious appetites. For these reasons, it's expensive to farm frogs and few operations have been successful.

FEWER DISSECTIONS

Every year there is less demand for wild-caught amphibians used for classroom dissections. In part this is because more animals are now being raised in laboratories for educational purposes. But another important factor is that teachers are becoming more aware that amphibians are declining. There's no need for every student to do a dissection (as was thought when I went to high school in the 1960s). Now, often the teacher will demonstrate a dissection for the class or have the students work in groups. Many states in the United States and many western European countries now have "dissection-choice" laws. Students are given the option of not dissecting animals. Argentina and the Slovak Republic have actually banned dissection of animals in high schools!

Now there are also alternatives to dissection. Videotapes of frog dissections can be used. CD-ROMs are available. You can dissect 3-dimensional frog models. And you can even go to the Web to www.froguts.com and dissect a frog by moving your mouse.

WISER HARVESTING OF WILD POPULATIONS

Some people think we should protect all wildlife. These people would support laws banning the killing of all animals in the name of conservation. Other people believe that it's their right to hunt whatever animals they want, and as many as they want. Conservation biologists believe that for many species of wildlife we can conserve them and also hunt them.

The key is that harvesting (removing animals from wild populations) must be done on a sustainable basis. *Sustainable harvesting* means removing individuals from a population in such a way that the population will be there long into the future. This might mean only taking a few individuals from the population, or only taking "extra" adult males and leaving the females.

Many conservation biologists support the harvest of wildlife on a sustainable basis because it gives countries an incentive to protect their wildlife and critical habitats. For example, because legally-caught crocodilian skins are worth a lot of money, many countries protect wetlands and carefully regulate hunting so that crocodilian populations are not wiped out. Every crocodile, alligator, or caiman is worth money!

How do we know which animals to remove and how many we can remove to practice sustainable harvesting? Only research can provide these answers. Biologists carry out long-term studies to determine the number of juveniles, subadults, and adults in a population. They study the causes of death and the chance of an individual surviving to maturity. They learn how many eggs a female produces during a breeding season and how often females breed per lifetime. Once armed with a good set of data, the biologists can make recommendations so that collecting or hunting can be done without causing the population to go extinct.

WHAT CAN YOU DO TO HELP?

When we think about all the ways that humans are responsible for the declines and disappearances of amphibians and reptiles, it's easy to become discouraged. But when we think about all the positive steps people are taking, or can take, to protect these animals, we have reason to be hopeful.

YOU can be part of the solution. *Conservation*-minded young adults are often more receptive to new ideas than are adults. YOU are the generation that can have a major impact on the future of amphibians and reptiles, beginning with the present. YOU will be the voters of tomorrow. YOU will be setting the policies of tomorrow. YOU will raise the children of tomorrow. YOU can make a difference.

Following are some ideas of things to do—and things not to do—to help amphibians and reptiles.

DON'T:

- Don't destroy habitat. Habitat modification and destruction are the major causes of declines and disappearances of amphibians and reptiles. If you're out in the woods looking for amphibians and reptiles, be sure to put the rocks and logs back in place after you've looked underneath them.

- Don't release exotic amphibians and reptiles into the environment. They might eat local amphibians and reptiles. Or they could survive and breed, eventually out-competing local amphibians and reptiles for food or habitat. Find someone who will care for the animals and enjoy them as you once did.

This comical-looking animal is a White's tree frog from Australia, commonly sold in pet stores. If one of these frogs got loose, it might eat smaller native tree frogs.

- Don't buy souvenirs made from amphibians and reptiles. Key chains made from rattlesnake rattles may look cool, but the rattles belong to the snakes. Cowboy boots made from tegu lizard skins are beautiful, but even more beautiful is a live tegu sunning itself on a log. You may be tempted to buy an exquisitely carved tortoiseshell comb in a foreign country. Don't. Not only was a sea turtle killed to make the comb, but it's also *illegal* to bring tortoiseshell into the United States. And don't eat sea turtle soup or the meat of any other *endangered* reptile. The less we support the exploitation of amphibians and reptiles, the fewer animals will be killed and made into cheap souvenirs or gourmet dishes.

DO :

- Do educate yourself about amphibians and reptiles. The more you learn about them, the more you'll appreciate them, and the more you'll want to protect them. Read. Your library has good books about these animals. If there's a herpetological club in your city, join it—it's a great way to meet other people who share your interests. Many local museums, zoos, and nature centers offer classes on amphibians and reptiles. Spend time outdoors observing amphibians and reptiles in their natural environment. Keep a field notebook and record your observations. You may discover something new.

- Do volunteer your time. Often scientists working in universities, museums, or nature centers use volunteer help to work with amphibians and reptiles. You can dig ponds for amphibians in areas where natural breeding ponds have been destroyed. During rainy spring and summer evenings you can help migrating amphibians and reptiles to cross roads safely.

- Do let people know that conserving amphibians and reptiles is important. You can improve the public image of these animals by letting others know how fascinating they are. Give talks to your classmates at school. Write letters to the editor for your local newspaper. Often when a *threatened species* is being considered for protection, the public is invited and encouraged to express their viewpoints. Write letters that express your opinions. Send the letters to your state and national representatives, and have all your friends add their signatures. The representatives may be impressed by your knowledge and interest.

- Do support conservation organizations. Begin by spending time in your library reading about the different conservation groups. Some buy land and preserve it. Others spend money to protect wildlife. Others fund research to study threatened and endangered species. Some do a combination of activities. Choose an organization whose goals and activities you most admire. Then ask your parents to give you a membership in your chosen organization. You'll receive a magazine or newsletter, providing you with information on con-servation projects and the status of threatened and endangered plants and animals.

- Do be responsible if you want to keep amphibians and reptiles as pets. Never take a threatened or endangered species from the wild. To find out which species are protected, contact a U. S. Fish and Wildlife Service officer. If you're buying an exotic animal from a pet store, ask if it was bred in captivity. Don't buy exotic animals that were taken from the wild. The fewer of these animals that are sold, the fewer will be shipped in future years. Find out about your pet's needs—food, water, habitat, and temperature and moisture con-ditions. And then provide them with the *best* substitute home you can for their entire lives.

- Do make your backyard a good place for amphibians and reptiles. Instead of having all grass, leave rocks or logs on the ground to serve as shelters. Urge your parents to use organic insecticides rather than toxins to kill the insect pests that eat your garden vegetables and flowers. This way the amphibians and reptiles in your yard won't die from eating poisoned insects. If you have a cat, keep it indoors or at least don't let it outside unsupervised. Cats are very efficient predators. They can wipe out the lizards in your neighborhood in no time.

If we all do our part to help protect the environment and the animals themselves, our grandchildren's grandchildren will be able to learn about amphibians and reptiles from watching them in the wild. If would be sad indeed if frogs, salamanders, caecilians, turtles, crocodilians, lizards, snakes, and tuatara joined the dinosaurs on the growing list of extinct animals. You and I together can make a difference. Please help.

Glossary

Words defined in the glossary are italicized in the text for their first appearance in each chapter.

Acid rain—rain that is acidic from pollutants, especially sulfuric acid and nitric acid

Adaptable—able to adjust to changes

Amnion—membrane that encloses a reptile embryo in fluid (bird and mammal embryos also have an amnion; fishes and amphibians do not)

Antivenin—substance that counteracts a snake's venom

Aquatic—living in the water

Arboreal—living in the trees

Camouflaged—blending in with the surroundings

Carapace—top part of a turtle's shell

Carnivorous—feeding on animal matter

Class—major division of subphylum used in scientific classification; amphibians belong to the class Amphibia; reptiles belong to the class Reptilia

Colonial nester—animal that gathers in a large group to lay its eggs

Conservation—protection and careful use of natural resources so that they will still be available far into the future

Conservation easement—agreement made between the government or a conservation organization and a landowner on how private land will be used; landowner often receives money or tax benefit in return for not developing the land

Deforestation—the cutting and clearing away of forests

Dewlap—throat fan in lizards; males spread out fan in display to females and other males

Direct development—all development takes place within the egg; instead of a larval stage, a miniature of the adult form hatches from the egg

Diurnal—active during the day

Ecotourism—tourism based on natural history

Ectothermic—depending on external (outside) source of heat to warm the body; generally the source of heat is the sun

Endangered—in danger of extinction throughout all or most of a species range

Endothermic—having built-in control of body temperature; producing heat chemically inside the body to maintain constant, high body temperature

Farming operation—animals are collected from the wild and bred in captivity; some of the captive-bred young are saved for future breeding, the rest are sold; does not require a continuing supply of animals taken from the wild

Head-starting—program of hatching eggs in captivity and then raising the young until they are large enough to be less vulnerable to predators; then, they are released into the wild

Herbivorous—feeding on plant matter

Herpetologist—scientist who studies amphibians and reptiles

Herpetology—the scientific study of amphibians and reptiles

Home range—area within which an animal moves about in its daily activities to find food and shelter

Invertebrate—animal without a backbone consisting of vertebrae (for example, worm, insect, spider)

Jacobson's organ—sense organ in the roof of a snake's mouth; detects chemicals

Keratin—hard protein substance found in scales of reptiles and scutes of turtles (and in birds' feathers and humans' fingernails)

Metamorphosis—process of transforming, or changing, from the larval body form to the adult body form

Nocturnal—active at night

Omnivorous—feeding on both plant and animal matter

Order—major subdivision of class used in scientific classification; Amphibia is divided into three orders; Reptilia is divided into four orders

Oviparous—egg-laying

Ozone—form of oxygen; the ozone layer blocks most of the ultraviolet (UV) radiation from striking the Earth's surface

Parotoid—gland located behind the eye on a toad; contains toxic secretion

Permeable skin—substances can enter and pass back out easily

Plastron—lower part of a turtle's shell

Poisonous—having toxin in the skin

Population—individuals of a species that live together and can mate with one another

Population density—number of individuals in a population

Ranching operation—eggs or hatchlings are taken from the wild and raised in captivity to be sold later; because adults are not bred in captivity, the operation requires a continuing supply of wild animals

Scutes—plates (made from keratin) that cover a turtle's shell

Specialized—able to survive only within a narrow set of environmental conditions

Species—all the individuals that could breed successfully with one another if they were all in the same place, but not with individuals of other species

Sustainable harvesting—removing (hunting or collecting) animals from a population in such a way that the population will still be there long into the future

Tail autotomy—ability to lose part of the tail voluntarily (many salamanders and lizards drop part of their tail as a defense against predators)

Terrestrial—living on land

Threatened—likely to become endangered within the near future

Venomous—having toxin in glands in the mouth; toxin is chewed or injected into prey or predator through teeth or fangs

Vertebrate—animal that has a backbone made up of vertebrae (for example, fish, amphibian, reptile, bird, mammal)

Viviparous—giving birth to live young (as opposed to laying eggs)

Vocal sac—pouch in the throat area of a male frog that fills with air when he calls

Main Sources Consulted

(in addition to over 100 scientific papers)

Cooksey, G. *Endangered Species: Must They Disappear?* Farmington Hills, MI: Information Plus Reference Series. Gale Group, 2001.

Duellman, William E. and Linda Trueb. *Biology of Amphibians.* New York: McGraw-Hill Book Company, 1986.

Greene, Harry W. *Snakes: The Evolution of Mystery in Nature.* Berkeley, CA: University of California Press, 1997.

Mattison, Chris. *Lizards of the World.* New York: Facts on File, 1989.

Miller, G. Tyler, Jr. *Living in the Environment.* Pacific Grove, CA: Brooks/ Cole Publishing Company, 2000.

Pough, F. Harvey, John B. Heiser, and William N. McFarland. *Vertebrate Life.* Upper Saddle River, NJ: Prentice Hall, 1996.

Pough, F. Harvey, Robin M. Andrews, John E. Cadle, Martha L. Crump, Alan H. Savitzky, and Kentwood D. Wells. *Herpetology.* Upper Saddle River, NJ: Prentice Hall, 2001.

Reading, R. P. and B. Miller, eds. *Endangered Animals: A Reference Guide to Conflicting Issues.* Westport, CT: Greenwood Press, 2000.

Stebbins, Robert C. and Nathan W. Cohen. *A Natural History of Amphibians.* Princeton, NJ: Princeton University Press, 1995.

World Resources 2000–2001: People and Ecosystems: The Fraying Web of Life. New York: Elsevier Science, 2000.

Further Resources:
Amphibians and Reptiles

BOOKS

Badger, David. *Frogs.* Stillwater, MN: Voyageur Press, Inc., 1995.

Baskin-Salzberg, Anita and Allen Salzberg. *Turtles.* New York: Franklin Watts, 1996.

Bauchot, Roland, ed. *Snakes: A Natural History.* New York: Sterling Publishing Co., Inc., 1994.

Behler, John L. *First Field Guide: Reptiles.* National Audubon Society. New York: Scholastic Inc., 1999.

Behler, John L. and Deborah A. Behler. *Alligators and Crocodiles.* Stillwater, MN: Voyageur Press, 1998.

Cassie, Brian. *First Field Guide: Amphibians.* National Audubon Society. New York: Scholastic Inc., 1999.

Clarke, Barry. *Eyewitness Books: Amphibian.* New York: Dorling Kindersley Publishing, Inc., 2000.

Greer, Allen E., consulting ed. *Reptiles.* Time-Life Books, 1996.

Halliday, Tim R. and Kraig Adler, eds. *The Encyclopedia of Reptiles and Amphibians.* New York: Facts on File, Inc., 1986.

Johnson, Sylvia A. *Tree Frogs.* Minneapolis, MN: Lerner Publications Company, 1986.

Johnston, Ginny and Judy Cutchins. *Slippery Babies: Young Frogs, Toads, and Salamanders.* New York: Morrow Junior Books, 1991.

Lamar, William W. *The World's Most Spectacular Reptiles & Amphibians.* Tampa, FL: World Publications, 1997.

Mattison, Chris. *Frogs & Toads of the World.* New York: Facts on File, 1987.

———. *Lizards of the World.* New York: Facts on File, 1989.

————. *Snake.* Ontario, Canada: Firefly Books Ltd., 1999.

————. *Snakes of the World.* New York: Facts on File, 1990.

McCarthy, Colin. *Eyewitness Books: Reptile.* New York: Alfred A. Knopf, 1991.

Owen, Oliver S. *Tadpole to Frog: Lifewatch. The Mystery of Nature.* Edina, MN: Abdo & Daughters, 1994.

Simon, Seymour. *Crocodiles and Alligators.* New York: HarperCollins Publishers, 1999.

————. *Snakes.* New York: HarperCollins Publishers, 1992.

Tesar, Jenny. *What on Earth Is a Tuatara?* Woodbridge, CT: Blackbirch Press, 1994.

WEB SITES

www.allaboutfrogs.org

Interesting, weird, and silly facts about frogs; declining amphibian populations; frogs as pets.

www.cgee.hamline.edu/frogs/science/frogfact.html

Information about amphibians, including population declines.

elib.cs.berkeley.edu/aw

Amphibian conservation and biology, including life history, geographic distribution, and photos.

www.bio.davidson.edu/Biology/herpcons/Kids/kids.html

Facts about amphibians and reptiles; backyard projects; what you can do to protect amphibians and reptiles.

www.froguts.com

Dissect a frog without killing an animal—move your mouse!

www.frogweb.gov/index.html

Amphibian declines and deformities.

www.homestead.com/kidstuff/index.html

Pet care, books and videos about frogs, miscellaneous facts about frogs.

www.naherpetology.org

Herpetological meetings, species, publications, links with other herpeto-logical web sites, careers in herpetology; focus is on the United States and Canada.

www.parcplace.org

Conservation and biology of amphibians and reptiles: threats, conserva-tion efforts, geographic distribution.

www.reptilemom.com

News and views about endangered turtles and snakes.

www.sdnhm.org/exhibits/reptiles

Some information refers to exhibits at the San Diego Natural History Museum, but there are also games and information about reptiles; field guides to many species around San Diego; list of books for teachers and kids.

www.starfish.ch/reef/reptiles.html

Marine reptiles: sea snakes and turtles.

Further Resources:
Conservation

BOOKS

Asimov, Isaac. *Why Are Animals Endangered?* Milwaukee, WI: Gareth Stevens, Inc., 1993.

———. *Why Are the Rain Forests Vanishing?* Milwaukee, WI: Gareth Stevens, Inc., 1992.

Bloyd, Sunni. *Endangered Species.* San Diego, CA: Lucent Books, 1989.

Challand, Helen J. *Disappearing Wetlands.* Chicago, IL: Children's Press, 1992.

———. *Vanishing Forests.* Chicago, IL: Children's Press, 1991.

Chandler, Gary and Kevin Graham. *Guardians of Wildlife.* New York: Twenty-First Century Books, 1996.

Duffy, Trent. *The Vanishing Wetlands.* New York: Franklin Watts, 1994.

Gallant, Roy A. *Earth's Vanishing Forests.* New York: Macmillan Publishing Company, 1991.

Hodgkins, Fran. *Animals Among Us: Living with Suburban Wildlife.* North Haven, CT: Linnet Books, 2000.

Hoyt, Erich. *Extinction A–Z.* Hillside, NJ: Enslow Publishers, Inc., 1991.

Levy, Charles. *Endangered Species—Crocodiles and Alligators.* Secaucus, NJ: Chartwell Books, 1991.

Mara, William P. *The Fragile Frog.* Morton Grove, IL: Albert Whitman & Company, 1996.

Mutel, Cornelia F. and M. M. Rodgers. *Our Endangered Planet: Tropical Rain Forests.* Minneapolis, MN: Lerner Publications Company, 1991.

Patent, Dorothy H. *Biodiversity.* New York: Clarion Books, 1996.

Phillips, Kathryn. *Tracking the Vanishing Frogs.* New York: St. Martin's Press, Inc., 1994.

Phillips, Pamela. *The Great Ridley Rescue.* Missoula, MT: Mountain Press, 1988.

Pringle, Laurence. *Saving Our Wildlife.* Hillside, NJ: Enslow Publishers, Inc., 1990.

Seibert, Patricia. *Toad Overload: A True Tale of Nature Knocked Off Balance in Australia.* Brookfield, CT: Millbrook, 1995.

Silver, Donald. *Why Save the Rain Forest?* New York: Julian Messner, 1993.

Stefoff, Rebecca. *Extinction.* New York: Chelsea House Publishers, 1992.

Tesar, Jenny. *Shrinking Forests.* New York: Facts on File, 1991.

Thomas, Peggy. *Reptile Rescue.* Brookfield, CT: Twenty-First Century Books, 2000.

Wolkomir, Joyce R. and Richard Wolkomir. *Junkyard Bandicoots and Other Tales of the World's Endangered Species.* New York: John Wiley & Sons, Inc., 1992.

WEB SITES

www.eco-pros.com

Focus is on environmental education; information about the environment and how you can protect it.

www.globalresponse.org/yea

Learn what you can do to become an environmental activist!

www.greenscreen.org

Facts, activities, and stories about the environment for kids; resources for teachers; newsletter—nature news, by kids for kids.

www.kidsforsavingearth.org

Environmental education: conservation, endangered species, ecological concerns. Find out what you can do to help.

www.yptenc.org.uk

Site designed to encourage young people's understanding of the environment; facts about animals and the environment; conservation.

Conservation Organizations

Conservation International
1919 M Street NW, Suite 600
Washington, DC 20036
Tel. 800-406-2306
www.conservation.org

Defenders of Wildlife
1101 14th Street NW, #1400
Washington, DC 20005
Tel. 202-682-9400
www.defenders.org

Environmental Defense Fund
257 Park Ave. S
New York, NY 10010
Tel. 212-505-2100
www.environmentaldefense.org

Friends of the Earth
1025 Vermont Ave. NW
Washington, DC 20005
Tel. 202-783-7400
www.foe.org

Greenpeace USA
1436 U Street NW
Washington, DC 20009
Tel. 202-462-1177
www.greenpeace.org

National Audubon Society
700 Broadway
New York, NY 10003-9562

Tel. 800-274-4201
www.audubon.org

National Resources Defense Council
40 W. 20th Street
New York, NY 10011
Tel. 212-727-2700
www.nrdc.org

National Wildlife Federation
8925 Leesburg Pike
Vienna, VA 22184
Tel. 703-970-4100
www.nwf.org

The Nature Conservancy
4245 North Fairfax Drive, Suite 100
Arlington, VA 22203–1606
Tel. 800-628-6860
www.tnc.org

Rainforest Action Network
221 Pine Street, Suite 500
San Francisco, CA 94104
Tel. 415-398-4404
www.ran.org

Rainforest Alliance
65 Bleeker Street
New York, NY 10012
Tel. 212-677-1900
www.rainforest-alliance.org

Sierra Club
85 2nd Street, 2nd Floor
San Francisco, CA 94105-3441
Tel. 415-977-5500
www.sierraclub.org

The Wilderness Society
900 17th Street NW
Washington, DC 20006
Tel. 202-833-2300
www.wildernesssociety.org

Wildlife Conservation Society
2300 Southern Boulevard
Bronx, NY 10460
Tel. 718-220-5100
www.wcs.org

World Wildlife Fund
1250 24th Street, NW
Washington, DC 20037
Tel. 800-225-5993
www.wwf.org

Worldwatch Institute
1776 Massachusetts Ave. NW
Washington, DC 20036
Tel. 202-452-1999
www.worldwatch.org

Index

Scientific names are listed only for representative species. Pages with photographs and illustrations appear in boldface type.

About the Author

Marty Crump raised tadpoles and kept garter snakes as pets when she was a kid. She has been a professional herpetologist for the past 34 years and has done research in Costa Rica, Brazil, Ecuador, Argentina, and Chile. Most of her research has focused on behavior and ecology of tropical frogs. Marty received her Ph.D. from the University of Kansas and is currently an Adjunct Professor of Biology at Northern Arizona University and a Conservation Fellow with the Wildlife Conservation Society. She is the 1997 recipient of the Herpetologists' League Distinguished Herpetologist Award. Marty wrote *In Search of the Golden Frog* (The University of Chicago Press, 2000), about her adventures as a field biologist working in Latin America, and is one of six coauthors of a college herpetology textbook (*Herpetology*. Pough et al. Prentice Hall, 2001). She has also written more than 50 scientific papers.

Marty watches marine iguanas on the Galápagos Islands.
Photo by Alejandro Grajal